IN MEMORY

Bill Cauble and Clifford Teinert respectfully dedicate this book to the memory of Watkins Reynolds Matthews, a true inspiration and mentor to both of us.

bright sky press
Albany, Texas

Copyright © 2002 by Bright Sky Press

10   9   8   7   6   5   4   3   2   1

Library of Congress Cataloging-in-Publication Data

Cauble, Bill, 1938–Barbecue, biscuits, and beans: chuck wagon cooking /
Bill Cauble and Cliff Teinert; foreword by Tommy Lee Jones.
p. cm.
ISBN 1-931721-40-8 (sftcvr: alk. paper)
1. Outdoor cookery. 2. Cookery, American--Western style.
I. Teinert, Cliff, 1939- II. Title.
TX823 .C337 2002
641.5'78--dc21
2002022657

BOOK AND COVER DESIGN BY: Tina Taylor
EDITED BY: Katie Dickie Stavinoha
PHOTOGRAPHY BY: Watt M. Casey, Jr.

Printed in China through Asia Pacific Offset

BARBECUE
BISCUITS & BEANS
CHUCK WAGON COOKING

BILL CAUBLE 🌶 CLIFF TEINERT

★ THAT WAS THEN ★

★ THIS IS NOW ★

CONTENTS

★

FOREWORD

by Tommy Lee Jones

Any means of transportation has underlying social implications. Automobiles have brought individual independence, national petrochemical dependency, and road rage to Americans. Genghis Khan conquered most of the civilized world when he mastered the use of horses to support his military endeavors. Railroads united the East and West Coasts of the United States. And the nuclear age began when a bomb was dropped from an airplane.

What about the Chuck Wagon?

People who follow migratory animals have always, like any people, needed to eat. At one time or another we could slay a mastodon or an elk and eat it where it lay. Sheep herders have always lived on their casualties. The chuck wagon, as we know it, was invented by Charlie Goodnight in the second half of the 19th century to support cattle drives from Texas to the railheads of the North—a formative socio-economic development of what Texans now call home. What did Charlie have in mind, and why is it relevant to us now?

From my point of view at the WD Ranch in Culberson and Jeff Davis Counties in West Texas, we use the chuck wagon for the same reason Charlie did, because we have to. We have to keep ten cowboys out from daylight to dark for two weeks in the fall and two weeks in the spring. The distances are great, and travel time in pickups away from the cattle and back, whether it be to the headquarters or to town, would cut our work day in half. Sandwiches stuffed in saddle bags could never meet our nutritional requirements for more than a day or two. The wagon provides three good meals a day and keeps us not only happy, but places us in our rightful historical perspective. By this I mean it makes us better hands. If we spend 30 minutes eating a beautiful meal off the wagon and go back to work, we will stress the cattle less and be less likely to get a horse or a man hurt than if we spent several hours on the road hunting fast food in the middle of the day.

Why should the wagon mean anything to anybody else? They are a lot of fun. Many people are reminded of Western movies and television shows. Other people are happy to see a part of their culture that hasn't died yet.

Clifford Teinert, Bill Cauble, and others like them have studied and tracked the techniques of chuck wagon cooking and, through this book, made them available to all. The backyard cook can improve greatly on the usual barbecue he serves his family and friends while keeping a good tradition alive. Nostalgia, like any other form of sentimentality, is dangerous and often fatal to culture. Insofar as you are interested in having a culture, you are invited to use this book for the right reason—because you have to.

CHUCK WAGON HISTORY

by Lawrence Clayton

To many people, two scenes epitomize the Old West. The first is a trail herd of Longhorn cattle strung out across a rolling landscape. The other is a chuck wagon with cowboys lounging around its smoky campfire while the crusty cook turns out sourdough biscuits, beans, fried beef and coffee. These two scenes were an authentic part of the Western experience. The wagon was the center of the cowboys' life where they slept, ate, doctored their ills and shared experiences; it symbolized home in a land where permanency was scarce.

While time has erased many of those wagons, a group of chuck wagon aficionados resurrected many details and provided authenticity. Bill Cauble and Clifford Teinert were original members of the group. Bill has been a ranch cook as well as a chuck wagon cook for many years. He has also rebuilt a wagon using the information on appropriateness of wood and hardware. Clifford has a long history of wagon cooking, even as a professional caterer of considerable reputation. He was the first person to act on the idea of catering from a chuck wagon and formed his Texas Trails Chuck Wagon Company in 1970.

Cauble, Teinert and others had watched the chili cookoffs take on the air of a circus with little or no effort to fit into any historically oriented tradition, if there was one to fit into. Chuck wagon cooking is different because there is strong tradition.

The revival of interest brought many amateurs into the cookoffs and other western-oriented events. Those amateurs outfitted their wagons with inappropriate homemade boxes. Too, variations from the authentic included menu items that would not have graced the sparse setting of the wagon cook's domain.

As a result of the efforts of Cauble, Teinert and others, the Western Chuck Wagon Association's purpose is to perpetuate the heritage of the trail drives, especially as reflected in the chuck wagons and Dutch oven cooking. To accomplish this goal, they've established guidelines to assist

people in achieving authenticity. An ultimate aim is to create a registry of authentic wagons to be housed at the National Cowboy and Western Heritage Museum, formerly known as the National Cowboy Hall of Fame. Each registered wagon would bear a bronze plaque featuring the mark of the Western Chuck Wagon Association and the museum.

Not only have questions about authenticity been answered by these traditionalists, but more information is available on what is and is not appropriate. These enthusiasts for authentic chuck wagons have influenced judging the appropriateness of wagons, chuck boxes and gear at contests in which the authentic is lauded and the spurious rejected.

It is pretty clear that the modern beliefs about the reality of trail camp and ranch cook are different in several respects from what was real.

The public will see what chuck wagons actually looked like and enjoy equally authentic camp surroundings. Our enjoyment should be greater and the historical accuracy enhanced by a group dedicated to the reality of the Old West.

Famous trail driver and rancher Charles Goodnight deserves credit for building the first authentic chuck wagon to accompany cowboys herding cattle up the trail. He used available materials and mechanical technology to create a model used for several decades before the chuck wagon became an essential for many Western ranches.

Sturdiness, not fanciness, marked the chuck wagons. They had to be able to withstand the rough treatment they received. Old army wagons were good choices because they were built to stand the test of time and use. But the wagon was only part of the required gear. The chuck box was the main focus.

There was no absolutely certain design, and there was a commonality that marked the real ones. The chuck box was constructed of lumber measuring 1" X 4" X 12', either planks or tongue-in-groove. Some beaded ceiling siding was used. The height of the boxes varied but was not so tall that the cook could not reach its top from the ground. Shelves were common, and so were drawers. Some were square, but the classic profile was a box as wide as the wagon bed, deeper at the bottom than at the top. The slanted covering had tin to protect it and to provide a durable surface on which the cook could roll out dough or work his other comestibles. When in a lowered position, the table was supported by one or two legs, or held in place by a piece of chain.

Garnet Brooks of El Reno, Oklahoma, described the authentic wagon and chuck box and the other items in a typical trail camp in the First Annual Old Time Chuck Wagon Round-Up and Cattlemen's Ball (1991). The wooden running

gear of the wagon ran on steel-bound wooden wheels. The rear wheel stood about 54 inches high and the front 45 inches high. The tires ranged from two to four inches in width. The wagons had a tongue, double tree, single trees, and neck yoke, all of iron-reinforced wood, usually oak. The cook rode on a spring seat and helped control his wagon with a brake assembly. The wagon bows that kept the canvas covering over the wagon's load consisted of four or five bows, the two end ones often made of the steel from an old wagon tire, the others of wood. The paint was usually green or light blue.

★ *A well-known author, Dr. Lawrence Clayton, who died in 2001, was committed to documenting the life of contemporary cowboys and preserving the history of ranching in Texas. He served as Dean at Hardin-Simmons University, and helped found Abilene's Western Heritage Classic.*

We both tend to cook by feel or memory...
but our wives have prodded us

into writing down measurements so
they can be replicated again and again.

BILL CAUBLE

★

Growing up the eldest of four boys, I was blessed with a mother who insisted that we make our beds and learn to cook. After trying the oilfields in West Texas and a stint as an artist, it was time to come home to Albany Texas.

I became the cook at the Lambshead Ranch which was managed by Watt Matthews. I cooked breakfast for the cowboys, Watt and his family, and a big lunch for whoever was near the cookshack. Regularly, and always unexpectedly, as many as 30 people would drive 20 miles to the ranch for dinner after Watt's impromptu invitation.

It's true that a cowboy has a simple life and simple tastes, but don't believe that a cowboy will eat just anything. It's got to be good and filling. If it is, they'll eat the same thing five days a week. I'm sure my experience as a ranch cook was little different than a chuck wagon cook 130 years ago. Cowboys like meat, beans, potatoes and bread. They like corn. Some will eat a green vegetable, especially if it's fried. They want Ranch dressing, even if it's from a bottle. Because of these limitations, it was a challenge to create meals they liked. I found out that I really liked experimenting.

That resulted in a new experiment, aided by Watt, who was also keenly interested in history. With his blessing, I rebuilt an old chuck wagon using authentic materials and methods. This new pastime resulted in my serving on the board and eventually as president of the Ranching Heritage Center in Lubbock. The Center's goal is to capture historical life on Texas ranches through its architecture, stories and memorabilia.

I no longer cook at Lambshead regularly, but am in charge of maintenance and equipment upkeep there. After cooking for cowboys and ranch guests for so long, I was asked by people to "cook" for other events. And they were really interested in chuck wagon cooking. It may have been a novelty at first, but after people ate our cooking, they knew it was simple but delicious.

Now I am not only cooking for the pleasure of the cowboys or my family, but I enjoy cooking with others who love to cook, who love history and who have a passion for mixing the two.

CLIFFORD TEINERT

★

Homemade egg noodles and fresh beef were staples in my home in Central Texas. All of my grandparents migrated from Germany to Texas in 1854, bringing with them German ways of life and cooking traditions. As you can expect, sausage-making was an important day in the Teinert family; neighbors came from all around to help out.

I moved to Albany to work on a relative's ranch, and ranching is an industry I'm proud to be a part of today. The area is fine ranching country and the locals are dedicated to preserving history. Like Bill, I was interested in the history of the ranching business and in chuck wagon cooking. Watt Matthews gave me the shell of an old wagon that I rebuilt, and in 1970 I began a catering business called Texas Trails Chuck Wagon Catering Co.

That business went along when the Albany Fandangle cast and crew performed for President and Mrs. Lyndon B. Johnson near Johnson City. I've had the opportunity to cook for U.S. Presidents Ronald Reagan and George H. W. Bush and Mexican President Juan Lopez Portillo. I've also hosted many cowboys and people interested in chuck wagon cooking through my involvement with chuck wagon cookoffs. That connection has allowed me to help preserve chuck wagon history and western heritage by serving on the board of directors at the National Cowboy and Western Heritage Museum in Oklahoma City, Oklahoma. And as a rancher who loves to cook, I know the beef business from hoof to table. I'm also interested in improving the beef that appears in

stores, so I've become active in several livestock associations and serve as a director of the Southwestern Livestock Show and Exhibition in Fort Worth.

No matter the business or group I'm involved with, cooking remains a big part of my life.

Throughout the years, my menu has grown from beef, beans and salad, to fish, New Mexican influences, and first-rate breads and desserts. Richard Bolt of the Pitchfork Ranch taught me about sourdough. I always have my sourdough crock on my kitchen counter. My expanded menu today is a result of collaborating with many good cooks over the years.

PARTNERS

★

With both of us rebuilding old wagons and watching interest in chuck wagon cooking take off, we became more concerned about the future and how accurately chuck wagons would be portrayed. As a result, we helped found the Western Chuck Wagon Association, whose contest regulations seek to uphold the authentic elements of the old chuck wagons. Today competitors may enter two different divisions: ranch wagons and trail wagons. The first division permits wood-burning stoves and other accoutrements of cooking in a camp moved only periodically. The latter is more demanding in disallowing anything that could not be carried on a long journey and moved daily. All gear has to be constructed in such a manner as to survive the trip.

Because of our love of this heritage and dedication to its future, we are both actively involved with the National Cowboy and Western Heritage Museum's annual Western Heritage event held each April. We take our chuck wagons to Oklahoma City, prepare food under the wagon's canopy and talk to people about what we've learned along the way.

And we prepare good, simple food that wows those who come by our wagon. It doesn't have to be complicated to be tasty, nor does simplicity detract from its elegance.

Elegant and chuck wagon fare may seem incompatible, but they are not mutually exclusive terms. A whole rib eye cooked over mesquite coals accompanied by grilled vegetables, light-as-air Ranch Rolls and followed by a version of Bread Pudding, is as classy as you can get. It's simple, but it's simply delectable. We'd never serve hot dogs at a black tie event, but a mesquite-cooked prime rib gets you nothing but rave reviews.

What we offer in this book are simple ways to prepare great meals. We provide instructions for cooking outside or inside. We both tend to cook by feel or memory, but our wives have prodded us into writing down measurements so our successes can be replicated again and again. As a result, these are tried-and-true recipes for your family or the next festivity you're planning.

SIMPLY BLACK TIE

★

Every four years during Presidential Inauguration activities, the Texas State Society hosts a Black Tie and Boots party. While it may be something of an oddity in Washington D.C., wearing starched jeans, boots, a dress hat and a tuxedo shirt and jacket won't draw any stares in Texas. Nor will the food we serve to those donning the Texas Tuxedo.

Whether it's a wedding or a fancy party, our food stands the taste test. With starched tablecloths and fine china, the Whole Rib Eye we present is an elegant way to impress your guests. With good beef, fresh vegetables and light-as-air Ranch Rolls, all it'll take to finish the soirée with a resounding cheer is Bread Pudding with one of our simply delectable sauces.

Our fare proves that it doesn't have to be complicated to be good. With time, good ingredients, and attention to detail, Simply Black Tie is simple to achieve.

A well-seasoned Dutch oven is a prize today,
as it was on the cattle drives of old.

BREAKFAST

Cast iron will last a lifetime. It conducts heat well and when cared for properly, cleans up easily. A well-seasoned Dutch oven is a prize today, as it was on the cattle drives of old. In fact, Bill Cauble and Clifford Teinert have Dutch ovens that are over 100 years old—evidence that good care and proper usage extend the life of a valuable utensil. Many of the breakfast dishes in this section call for cooking in a Dutch oven or a cast iron skillet. But cast iron isn't just for breakfast, as you will see in later sections.

Chile
Eggs

You can make this the night before and serve a crowd the next morning.

10 eggs
1 pint cottage cheese
8 ounces Monterey Jack cheese, grated
$^1/_2$ stick butter
4 poblano peppers, roasted, peeled and chopped
2 jalapeños, seeded and chopped

Sift together:
$^1/_2$ cup flour
$^1/_2$ teaspoon salt
1 tablespoon baking powder

Preheat oven to 350º.

Beat eggs; combine with sifted ingredients. Add cheeses, butter and chiles. Mix well. Pour into 9 x 13-inch Pyrex or nonstick dish. Bake for 40 minutes or until center is set and lightly browned.

Cut into squares and serve with salsa, avocado or Chorizo Borracho, *recipe page 30.*

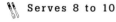 **Serves 8 to 10**

Tissa's Dutch Oven
Breakfast

Very good for Sunday morning brunch or Sunday supper.

2 tablespoons extra virgin olive oil
1 cup chopped onion
$^1/_2$ sweet red pepper, chopped
6 ounces chicken breast, cut into bite-sized pieces
8 ounces spicy pork sausage, cut into bite-sized pieces
1 to 2 tablespoons fresh rosemary, chopped
2 tablespoons dry red wine
10 large eggs
1$^1/_2$ cups cooked rice
1 teaspoon salt
$^1/_2$ teaspoon freshly ground black pepper
$^1/_2$ cup finely chopped fresh basil

Preheat oven to 375º.

Heat 14-inch Dutch oven or large oven-proof skillet over medium heat and add oil. Sauté onion, red pepper, chicken and sausage until vegetables are soft and meat is thoroughly cooked, about 10 minutes. Stir in rosemary and wine. Sauté for two minutes.

Turn heat to high. Whisk together eggs, rice, salt, pepper and basil. When oil begins to smoke, pour egg mixture into Dutch oven on top of vegetable and meat mixture. Remove Dutch oven from heat and stir slightly to disperse ingredients evenly. Bake 45 minutes or until center is firm. Cool at least 15 minutes.

You may cut into wedges and serve, or invert onto a platter.

 **Serves 4 to 6**

Dutch Oven
Eggs

Annually, Albany's Nail Ranch hosts a Western Hunt the first weekend of deer season. Hunters camp out under the stars and eat from the chuck wagon. To feed this crowd, this recipe is doubled. It's a great meal for a large group of people.

3 pounds potatoes, grated
1 cup diced yellow onion
1 red bell pepper, chopped
12 eggs
1/4 cup sharp Cheddar cheese, grated
1 pound bacon, diced

Preheat oven to 350°.

Brown bacon in large skillet. Sauté onions and peppers with browned bacon. Transfer to paper towel and set aside.

Brown potatoes, in bacon drippings, stirring constantly. Place on paper towel to absorb grease. Mix potatoes, bacon, onions and bell pepper and put into a 14-inch cake pan or oven-proof baking dish. Make 6 pockets in the mixture around perimeter of pan. Break 2 eggs into each pocket. Cover and bake about 15 minutes. Just before done, sprinkle cheese over eggs and continue baking until eggs are set.

Serve with Pico de Gallo, *recipe page 123*

 Serves 6

Skillet
Scramble

This is an easy, one-pan meal. We serve it to big groups of hunters, cowboys and family members with Sourdough Biscuits or Flour Tortillas. We think the best lean, thick-sliced bacon is made by Wright Brand Foods in Vernon, Texas.

2 pounds thick-sliced bacon, diced
1 pound pork sausage, crumbled
1 1/2 cups diced yellow onion
2 large tomatoes, chopped
1 jalapeño, diced but not seeded
1 tablespoon parsley, chopped
18 eggs
salt and pepper
1 cup sharp Cheddar cheese

Place diced bacon and crumbled sausage in hot 16-inch Dutch oven or large skillet on stove; cook until done. Pour off half of the drippings.

Combine onion, jalapeño and one of the tomatoes with pork mixture; sauté until onion is soft. Break eggs into bowl but do not beat. Pour eggs into cooked mixture and season with salt and pepper to taste. Break egg yolks with wooden spoon and stir continuously until eggs are nearly done.

Sprinkle top with remaining tomatoes, parsley and cheese. Cover for 2 to 3 minutes, and then serve directly to plates.

Serves 12 to 14

Breakfast
Potatoes

When Bill's mother fried sweet potatoes for four hungry boys, they became an instant success. Today, we'll mix sweets with whites when frying.

3 cups sweet potatoes, peeled and sliced crosswise in $1/8$-inch slices
3 cups white potatoes, peeled and sliced crosswise in $1/8$-inch slices
1 tablespoon kosher salt or sea salt
1 tablespoon chili powder or cayenne pepper
vegetable oil

In large skillet with $3/4$ to 1 inch of vegetable oil, fry potatoes in batches until golden brown, turning once. Drain each batch on paper towels. Sprinkle with salt while hot. Prior to serving, sprinkle with chili powder and/or cayenne pepper. Serve hot.

 **Serves 6 to 8**

Sourdough Whole Wheat Pancakes

Sourdough Whole
Wheat Pancakes

While sitting around a campfire one evening, somebody asked for pancakes. With sourdough and whole wheat, this recipe was born. It's a success every time.

4 cups Sourdough Starter, *recipe page 39*
1 cup whole wheat flour
2 eggs, beaten
$1/2$ cup sugar
2 tablespoons baking powder
$1/4$ to $1/2$ cup milk

Mix all ingredients except milk in medium mixing bowl. Add just enough milk to reach desired consistency; add more milk for a thinner pancake, less for thicker. Let rest for 15 to 20 minutes. Cook on hot, oiled griddle.

Serve with warm maple syrup and butter.

 Yields 12 to 15 pancakes

Homemade
Breakfast Sausage

Clifford's Uncle Marvin always used postage scales to measure his sausage spices. Any scale will do.

10 pounds ground pork
1 ounce black pepper
2 ounces salt

Mix salt and pepper. Spread ground pork on clean surface; sprinkle seasoning over the meat. Place in meat grinder and grind to fine texture. Place in large bowl and mix again by hand. Stuff in natural sausage casings, 24 inches long and 1 inch in diameter. Once a casing is stuffed, separate sausage in middle to allow a twist in the casing to form two links.

To smoke, place in smokehouse with low oak smoke running through for 8 hours. If you don't have access to a smokehouse, place oak bark, soaked in water, in a 1-gallon can and build a fire with a few pieces of dry oak bark. Place the can in the barbecue pit. Then place the sausage in the pit. Keep the bark from flaming up by keeping the pit tightly closed. Smoke slowly for 4 to 6 hours.

To cook, place link in skillet with $1/2$ inch of water to steam for 20 minutes.

 Yields 10 pounds sausage

Chorizo
Borracho

Borracho means drunken in Spanish. Roll this freshly cooked chorizo in a hot tortilla and have breakfast-on-the-run.

1 pound lean ground beef
1 pound ground pork
4 tablespoons chili powder
1 tablespoon black pepper
1 teaspoon salt
1 teaspoon ground cumin
2 cloves garlic, crushed
1 jigger or 1 ounce tequila

Combine all ingredients in a bowl and mix thoroughly. Place in ziplock bag and refrigerate 2 to 3 hours or overnight to allow flavors to blend with meat. Or use immediately.

When ready to prepare, form into patties and fry until done.

 Serves 6

In cowboy country, breakfast is the most important meal of the day next to dinner, which is at noon!

Huevos Especiales
Chorizo Chile Colorado

This recipe is the result of two cooks in the kitchen coming up with new ideas.

1 1/2 **cups West Texas Basic Red Chile Sauce warmed,**
recipe page 120
3/4 **cup cooked and crumbled Chorizo Borracho,**
recipe page 30
3/4 **cup cooked and crumbled bacon**
1/2 **cup chopped tomato**
1/2 **cup chopped onion**
1/2 **cup grated cheese**
1 **dozen eggs, freshly beaten**

Combine all ingredients except eggs and cheese.

In a heavy nonstick pan, scramble eggs over medium heat and turn out onto a warmed platter.

Pour the warm sauce mixture over the hot scrambled eggs. Top with the grated cheese and serve with hot flour tortillas.

 Serves 6

Cowboy Hall of Fame
Breakfast for 20

Annually since 1990, the National Cowboy and Western Heritage Museum in Oklahoma City puts on a two–day heritage fest showcasing the history of the American cowboy. We've been cooking at the breakfast event since the very first year. This dish is a favorite with all.

Folks will stampede to get to this colorful, tasty breakfast.

3 pounds diced bacon
2 pounds crumbled sausage
3 dozen eggs
4 cups chopped green onions
4 chopped tomatoes
1 pound shredded Cheddar cheese
3 dozen warmed flour tortillas
4 jalapeños, seeded and chopped
**extra whole jalapeños and several sprigs
of cilantro for garnish**

In a 20-inch skillet or 16-inch Dutch oven, fry bacon; set aside to drain. Add sausage to skillet, crumble it as it fries. Remove sausage, set aside to drain. Add onions to skillet and fry until just softened. Add eggs and scramble; once scrambled, push the eggs to the edge of the skillet. Just inside the ring of eggs, arrange the sausage. Continue adding bacon, onions and tomatoes. Leave a hole in the center for the jalapeños.

Decorate the pan with cilantro leaves and a few extra whole jalapeños.

Serve with piping-hot flour tortillas.

Folks will stampede
to get to this colorful,
tasty breakfast.

 Serves up to 20

Poblano Peppers

Serrano Chiles

Eggs with
Green Chiles

Easy to prepare and striking to serve. The chiles add color, as well as a little kick, to your morning meal.

2 to 4 rounded tablespoons chopped green chiles, Anaheims or poblanos
3 tablespoons butter
4 eggs
salt and pepper to taste

In skillet, sauté chopped chiles in butter for 2 to 3 minutes over moderate heat.

Break eggs into saucer and slide into the hot butter. Fry over moderate heat, basting with hot butter 'til desired doneness.

Salt and pepper to taste. Serve immediately.

Serves 2

Breakfast
Strata

Cowboys love this. Since it's made ahead, it's
a good dish to carry to another location to cook.

10 to 12 slices bread, trimmed and cubed
12 ounces grated sharp Cheddar cheese
6 to 7 eggs, lightly beaten
2 cups diced ham or sausage, cooked
2 tablespoons minced onion
3^2/$_3$ to 4 cups milk
1 teaspoon dry mustard
salt and pepper to taste

Preheat oven to 325°.

Put bread into buttered 9 x 13-inch dish. Sprinkle meat over
the bread. Cover with cheese. Combine remaining ingredients
and pour over. Refrigerate for 12 to 24 hours.

Bake for 1 hour or until knife inserted in center comes out
clean.

 **Serves 6 to 8**

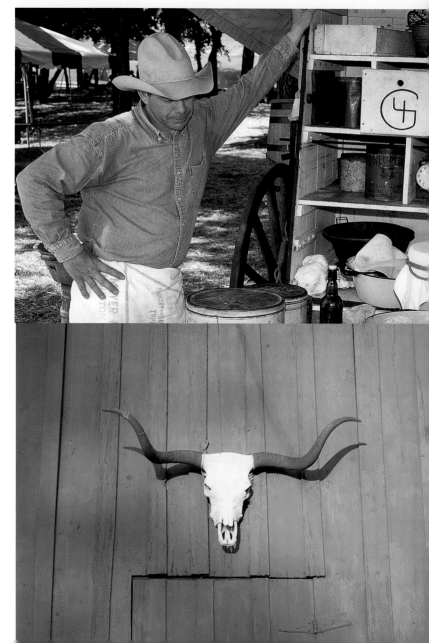

Sourdough starter—a true chuck wagon staple!

BREADS

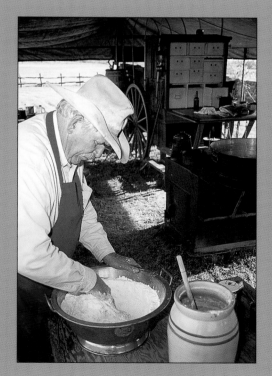

ourdough bread was a staple on the cattle trails and on ranches. Sourdough starter—the most important ingredient—easily adapts to today's kitchens. Crockery provides great storage, whether it's on your kitchen counter—as it is in Clifford Teinert's home kitchen—or in the refrigerator.

But don't let sourdough starter freeze. Chuck wagon cooks on the trail drives often took the sourdough crock to bed with them on cool nights. Their body warmth kept the starter from freezing and ruining. In this and the Desserts section, you'll find many recipes begin with sourdough.

Sourdough Biscuits

Sourdough
Starter

The secret to a good starter is to use often and keep fresh. Richard Bolt jokingly told us: "Keep two bullfrogs in your starter to keep it worked up."

1 2-ounce cake yeast or 3 $\frac{1}{4}$-ounce packets dry yeast
4 cups warm water
2 tablespoons sugar
4 cups all-purpose flour
1 raw potato, peeled and quartered

Dissolve yeast in warm water. Add sugar, flour and potato. Mix in crock and let rise until very light and slightly aged.

To remix starter, add 1 cup warm water, 2 teaspoons sugar and the amount of flour to mix to consistency of first starter. Set aside until biscuit time again. Never add yeast after the first time, but keep raw potato in as food for the starter. For best results, use daily. Store in refrigerator.

The closer the biscuits are crowded in the pan, the higher they will rise.

Sourdough
Biscuits

This recipe was passed along by Richard Bolt—for more than 40 years the cook at the famous Pitchfork Ranch. Richard knew more about the old ways of cooking than just about anyone. He even wrote his own cookbook *40 Years Behind the Lid.*

4 cups Sourdough Starter
4 cups all-purpose flour, sifted
1 teaspoon salt
2 tablespoons sugar
3 teaspoons, heaping, baking powder
4 tablespoons shortening

Preheat oven to 350°.

In a large bowl, form a nest or hollow in 4 cups of sifted flour. Pour 4 cups of Sourdough Starter into hollow. Add salt, sugar, baking powder and shortening. Mix well to form soft dough.

Pinch off in balls the size of an egg and place in well-greased 14-inch Dutch bread oven or skillet. Cast iron containers give the best results. Grease tops of biscuits generously. Set them in a warm place to rise for 5 to 10 minutes before baking.

Bake for 30 minutes or until nicely browned. The closer the biscuits are crowded in the pan, the higher they will rise.

When cooking in a covered Dutch oven over coals, consistent heat for baking sourdough biscuits is very important. Beware of wind and drafts, which can result in uneven heat.

 Yields 30 biscuits

Ranch
Rolls

This dough may be refrigerated for three or four days so that you can make as many or as few rolls as you need.

5 cups all-purpose flour
2 2-ounce cake yeast or 6 $1/4$-ounce packets dry yeast
$1/2$ cup sugar
$1/2$ cup vegetable oil
2 cups buttermilk
$1/2$ cup warm water
$1/2$ teaspoon soda
4 teaspoons baking powder
1 teaspoon salt

Preheat oven to 450°.

Dissolve yeast in warm water; let stand 10 minutes. Mix all dry ingredients. Add yeast mixture, oil and buttermilk. Stir with wooden spoon. Turn onto floured surface and knead lightly. Roll out and cut into 2-inch rolls. Generously oil top and bottom of rolls. Bake in 2- to 3-inch deep pan 12 to 15 minutes until golden.

This recipe will make 3 dozen rolls; unused dough may be refrigerated and used as needed.

TIP: Wooden spoons are preferred—buy the heaviest you can find—because you don't have to worry about them scratching stainless bowls or cast iron skillets.

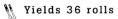 Yields 36 rolls

Ranch Rolls

Baking Powder
Biscuits

Baking powder was a staple on the chuck wagon and in all early kitchens. Our mothers often made these twice a day. They're good hot or cold.

2 cups all-purpose flour
3 teaspoons baking powder
$1/2$ teaspoon kosher salt or sea salt
6 tablespoons shortening or lard
$3/4$ cup milk

Preheat oven to 450°.

Mix flour, baking powder and salt in round-bottomed bowl. Cut shortening or lard in with pastry cutter until it resembles coarse meal. Stir in milk until dough forms a ball. Turn dough onto lightly floured surface and knead lightly. Roll or press with hands to about $1/2$-inch thickness. Cut with 2-inch biscuit cutter. Place on ungreased baking sheet, sides touching, and cook until light brown, usually 12 to 15 minutes.

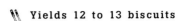 **Yields 12 to 13 biscuits**

Butter
Biscuits

Don't crowd these biscuits as you prepare them for the oven. They'll touch as they rise during cooking. Too, you may freeze uncooked biscuits and use as needed. When you bake them straight from the freezer, allow 18 to 20 minutes to cook.

2 cups all-purpose flour
1 cup whole wheat flour
3 tablespoons sugar
1 tablespoon baking powder
1 teaspoon salt
1 teaspoon baking soda
1 cup butter
1 $1/4$-ounce packet dry yeast
$1/4$ cup warm water
2 cups buttermilk
$3/4$ cup butter, melted

Preheat oven to 400°.

Combine the dry ingredients and sift together in a mixing bowl. With pastry blender, cut in butter until mixture resembles coarse meal. Dissolve yeast in warm water. Add to dry ingredients with the buttermilk. Blend thoroughly. Turn out on board dusted with wheat flour and roll or pat to $1/4$-inch thickness. Cut out with $2 1/2$-inch cutter. Dip biscuit in melted butter; fold in half. Bake on nonstick baking sheet for 15 minutes.

 **Yields 5 dozen**

Buttermilk
Biscuits

Biscuits are good with any meal—especially one where gravy, cooking juices or sauces are served. These light biscuits go really well with fried chicken or chicken-fried steak. The trick to making light-as-air biscuits is to work the dough as little as possible.

2 cups all-purpose flour
5 teaspoons baking powder
$^1/_2$ teaspoon salt
2 teaspoons sugar
$^1/_4$ cup shortening
$1^1/_4$ cups buttermilk

Preheat oven to 450°.

Let buttermilk reach room temperature. Mix dry ingredients. Cut in shortening. Stir in buttermilk. Roll out on floured surface about $^1/_2$ inch thick, and cut with biscuit cutter. Bake on nonstick pan, sides touching, for 10 to 12 minutes.

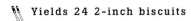 **Yields 24 2-inch biscuits**

The trick to making light-as-air biscuits
is to work the dough as little as possible.

Jalapeño
Cornbread

Many thanks to the late Ethel Casey for this cornbread. Serve with the Clear Fork Chili, *recipe page 71.*

1¹/2 cups cornmeal
2 cups corn, cut from cob and cooked
¹/4 cup sour cream
¹/3 cup shortening, melted
¹/2 cup onion, chopped
2 eggs, beaten
1 tablespoon baking powder
1 tablespoon sugar
1¹/2 cups sharp Cheddar cheese, grated
³/4 cup milk
¹/2 teaspoon baking soda
1 teaspoon salt
¹/2 cup seeded and chopped jalapeños

Preheat oven to 400°.

Mix all ingredients except jalapeños and cheese. Pour half of the batter into greased 9 x 9-inch baking pan. Sprinkle half of the cheese and jalapeños over batter. Pour remaining batter and top with remaining cheese and jalapeños. Bake at 400° for 45 minutes.

Double recipe to cook in 14-inch Dutch oven.

 Serves 6

Cornmeal
Rolls

These cornmeal rolls are unique and interesting in texture with the combination of meal and flour. These are great with butter and honey.

1¹/4 cups cornmeal
3 cups flour
¹/4 cup honey
4 teaspoons baking powder
¹/2 teaspoon soda
1 teaspoon salt
1³/4 cups buttermilk
¹/2 cup oil
3 ¹/4-ounce packets dry yeast
¹/2 cup warm water

Preheat oven to 425°.

Dissolve yeast in warm water; let rest 8 to 10 minutes. Mix all dry ingredients in large bowl. Pour in yeast and water. Using a wooden spoon, mix in oil, honey and buttermilk. Sprinkle flour over, just enough to be worked with your hands, and knead lightly. Pinch off egg-sized pieces and roll lightly in hands. Flatten rolls out and coat on both sides with oil. Bake in a 2- to 3-inch deep baking pan or ovenproof skillet generously coated with oil. Bake 15 to 18 minutes until brown.

 Yields about 20 large rolls

Best Basic
Cornbread

The best cornbread has a crusty bottom and sides. This is attained by heating your pan before placing the batter in it. For variety, add ¼ cup finely diced onion and 1 finely chopped jalapeño.

1 cup cornmeal
1 cup flour
4 teaspoons baking powder
½ teaspoon salt
1 cup milk
1 egg
¼ cup shortening
vegetable oil

Preheat oven to 425°.

Cover bottom of 9-inch round or square pan or 9-inch cast iron skillet with vegetable oil. Place oiled pan in the oven while mixing cornbread batter and heat until it just starts to smoke, about 5 to 7 minutes. Mix cornmeal, flour, baking powder and salt in a bowl. Add milk, egg and shortening. Mix with wooden spoon until blended. Pour mixture into hot pan or skillet. Bake for 20 to 25 minutes.

Cut into squares or wedges. Serve with plenty of butter.

 Serves 8

Mozelle Howsley's Monkey Bread

Mozelle Howsley's
Monkey Bread

Lynne Teinert's grandmother, Mozelle Howsley, said this is the "best monkey bread recipe ever."

3 cups all-purpose flour
2 cups milk, scalded
2 2-ounce cake yeast or 3 ^{1}/$_4$-ounce packets dry yeast
^{1}/$_2$ cup sugar
^{1}/$_2$ cup potato water
^{1}/$_2$ cup butter
2 teaspoons baking powder
^{1}/$_2$ teaspoon baking soda
1 teaspoon salt
^{1}/$_2$ cup mashed potatoes

Preheat oven to 350º.

Mix yeast and potato water that has been cooled to luke-warm, just warm enough to dissolve yeast. (Potato water is the water in which you have cooked potatoes.) Add milk, sugar, melted butter, mashed potatoes, baking powder, baking soda and salt. Mix until blended. Add flour and knead 10 minutes. Let rise twice. Roll out to ^{1}/$_2$-inch thickness; cut with knife into 2-inch squares. Dip squares in butter and place in 9-inch round tube pan. Bake for 35 to 40 minutes.

Yields two 9-inch ring loaves

Watt's
Hushpuppies

Many a convivial evening at the William Reynolds camp on the Clear Fork of the Brazos River has featured this quick, easy recipe. Watt Matthews and Millie Diller would make hush-puppies while John Bennett would fry freshly caught catfish. Use 1 teaspoon of salt for every cup of cornmeal. For a variation, add chopped jalapeños to cornmeal and salt mixture.

cornmeal
salt
boiling water
pan of cold water to wash and cool hands
vegetable oil

Combine cornmeal and salt in mixing bowl. Add just enough boiling water to soften. Very carefully pat out into 2 x ^{1}/$_4$-inch patties. Place on wax paper until ready to fry.

Fry in hot oil to cover.

**Yields approximately 8 hushpuppies
for each cup of cornmeal**

Zucchini
Bread

When the garden is running over, this is a great way to use zucchini.

3 eggs
$^{1}/_{2}$ teaspoon baking powder
1 cup vegetable oil
2 cups sugar
2 cups grated raw zucchini
2 teaspoons vanilla, divided
3 cups flour
1 teaspoon soda
1 teaspoon salt
$1^{1}/_{4}$ teaspoons cinnamon
1 cup pecans or walnuts, chopped

Preheat oven to 325°.

Combine eggs, oil and sugar. Beat until fluffy. Fold in zucchini and 1 teaspoon of vanilla. Add remaining ingredients and mix well. Pour into two greased and sugared loaf pans. Bake for about 1 hour or until straw inserted in middle comes out clean.

 Yields 2 loaves

There's no doubt that cowboys' tastes have changed in the past 20 years.

Flour
Tortillas

There's no doubt that cowboys' tastes have changed in the past 20 years. Flour tortillas and jalapeños are as much a staple as biscuits and gravy. This recipe is quick and easy, and you can use it to make fresh tortillas every day.

1 teaspoon salt
1/2 cup shortening
2 cups flour
1/2 teaspoon baking powder
boiling water

Add salt and baking powder to flour; work in shortening. Add just enough boiling water to make a stiff dough; knead until elastic. Let set 2 hours. Pinch off in small balls and roll into thin, flat rounds. Cook on ungreased griddle on top of stove.

Yields 12

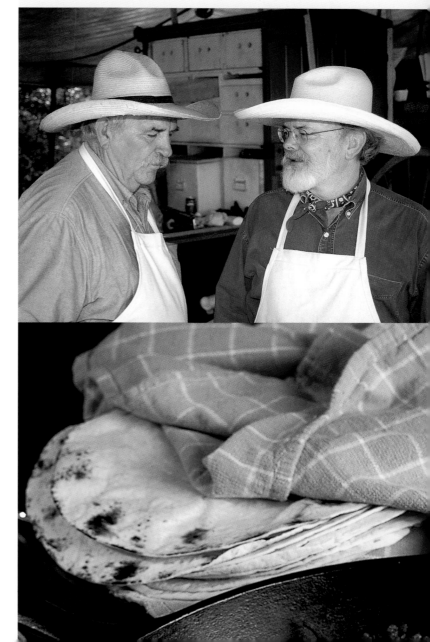

Flour Tortillas *(below)*

Don't let those mesquite coals go to waste.

MAIN DISHES

Why let those good mesquite coals in the fireplace go to waste? After the fire has burned down, spread the coals out and place a grill above them, at least 12 inches, depending on the amount of ashes. When grill is hot, throw on a well-seasoned rib eye or T-bone steak. Or you can use your Dutch oven in the fireplace by scooping hot coals on top of the oven, taking care to keep an even temperature.

BEEF & GAME

When you've touched and felt beef as it cooks many times, you can tell different degrees of doneness by the change in the firmness of the meat.

Beef
Tenderloin

Beef tenders are always a favorite in the ranching country.

2 beef tenderloins, well trimmed, about 3 pounds each
2 tablespoons freshly ground pepper
Brisket Rub, *recipe page 59*

In long pan to accommodate tenderloins, mix one portion of Brisket Rub with black pepper. Roll tenderloins in rub until all sides are equally coated. Cover with towel and bring tenderloins to room temperature. Roll meat in rub again before putting on your pit.

Cook on medium heat, rolling to brown all sides. Cook 1 to 1½ hours for medium rare (135°). Remove from pit and let rest 15 minutes before serving. This can be cooked 2 to 3 hours ahead and wrapped in aluminum foil and kept at room temperature. Meat will cook an additional 10 to 15°.

When cooking a single tenderloin, cook on the steak grill, 6 to 8 inches above hot coals. Watch carefully, turning frequently, about 40 to 45 minutes, until internal temperature reaches 140° for medium rare and 150° for medium. Remove from grill and let meat rest for 10 minutes before carving.

To cook in home kitchen, preheat oven to 350°.

Follow instructions for coating meat with Beef Rub. Roast for approximately 30 minutes until internal temperature reaches 140° for medium rare and 150° for medium. Remove from oven and let meat rest for 10 minutes before carving. Slice and serve.

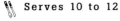 **Serves 10 to 12**

FEEL YOUR BEEF

It's a shame to cut into a steak or to stick a meat thermometer in to tell if it's cooked correctly. Punctures let that good juice run out and tend to dry the meat. Do it if you have to, but we swear by the "touch" method. When a steak is raw, it feels like jelly when you slightly jiggle it. As it cooks, it will firm up. If it doesn't shake at all, it's medium. Do this often enough and you'll learn how to "feel" the doneness of your steaks or tenderloins. Of course, if we're doing whole rib eyes or prime ribs, we'll use a thermometer.

Whole
Rib Eye

Some may be accustomed to calling this a rib eye roast, but cooked whole and then sliced is our preferred preparation. When you order a whole rib eye, it comes "lip on." After cooking, we slice the lip off and one of our favorite canine pets has a good supper.

When you've done this many times, you can tell different degrees of doneness by the change in the firmness of the meat. To be perfectly sure, use a meat thermometer.

14- to 15-pound whole rib eye–lip on
2 quantities Brisket Rub, *recipe page 59*
4 tablespoons freshly ground black pepper

In a pan large enough to hold the rib eye, place it fat side down. Coat generously with Brisket Rub and freshly ground black pepper. Roll meat and coat fat side. Pat rub and pepper onto the ends.

Place over medium-hot coals—30 to 32 inches above coals. Using clean gloves or thick cloth, turn rib eye once or twice, never cooking it very long with fat side down. When cooking several Whole Rib Eyes, you may use a large fork, but only pierce the fatty lip with the fork—never the meat. Allow 4 hours for medium rare (140°) and 4 1/2 hours for medium (160°).

When meat has reached desired temperature, take off coals and let rest 10 minutes. Cut lip off before serving. Slice into 3/4-inch slices and serve.

To cook in home kitchen, preheat oven to 350°.

Roast for 3 1/2 to 4 1/2 hours, until internal temperature reaches 140° for medium rare, and 160° for medium. Remove from oven and let rest for 10 minutes. Remove lip before serving.

Serves 15 to 20
depending on thickness of each serving

Brisket

Brisket

Brisket is a favorite at barbecue joints and picnics. The key to success is not for the faint-hearted or impatient. The best brisket is cooked over coals, not a live flame. Flames may produce impurities from the wood that enter the meat—you'll get a bright pink smoke ring, but it may be accompanied by a lingering aftertaste. Mesquite is our preferred wood, but others may be substituted.

We also stand by our mopping technique. We use a clean wash cloth or rag, taking care that no strings hang down. We tie a piece of wire around the cloth to transfer the mopping sauce to the meat. Some may feel more comfortable using a long-handled brush.

1 brisket, 7 to 11 pounds

Coat brisket with Brisket Rub, *recipe page 59,* especially on lean side.

Brisket should be cooked 12 to 13 hours at a constant 200° temperature until the brisket reaches 180° on meat thermometer. If cooking over live coals, cooking time may require 14 to 15 hours due to temperature fluctuations.

Mop with Brisket Mopping Sauce, *recipe page 59,* each time the brisket is turned; keep the mopping sauce on the pit to warm. Do not mop the last 2 hours of cooking.

Serves 8 to 10

Brisket Mopping Sauce

Brisket tends to become dry sometimes when cooked over live coals. This mopping sauce enhances the flavor and juiciness.

1 cup apple cider vinegar
1 cup vegetable oil
1 cup red wine, Burgundy or Chianti
2 cups water
2 sliced lemons
1 sliced onion
2 cloves garlic
1 tablespoon chili powder
1 tablespoon freshly ground black pepper
1 teaspoon kosher salt or sea salt

In saucepan, bring all ingredients to a boil. Remove from heat and use to mop brisket.

Yields 5 cups—
enough to mop and cook one brisket

Brisket Rub

Everyone has his own favorite, but this one works for us.

2 tablespoons freshly ground black pepper
1 tablespoon kosher salt or sea salt
1 teaspoon garlic powder
1 teaspoon onion powder
1 teaspoon dried parsley
1 tablespoon chili powder
1 teaspoon oregano
1 teaspoon sugar

Thoroughly mix all ingredients and rub on brisket. May double or triple amount and store in dry container for two to three weeks.

Yields 1/2 cup—enough to rub one brisket

The best brisket is cooked over coals, not live flames.

Steak Gravy

Leave about 1/4 cup oil and browned bits in skillet.
Add enough flour to absorb oil, approxiamtely 1/4
cup. Stirring constantly, add milk, about 4 cups, and
continue stirring until gravy reaches a smooth consistency. Thicker is usually preferred. Add 1 teaspoon
freshly ground pepper. Remove from heat and serve,
or keep warm and stir again before serving.

Chicken-Fried
Steak with Gravy

Double-dipping the steaks before frying gives
the best results and makes lots of flavorful
browned bits for your gravy-making.

**7 to 8 pounds cubed steak or lean round steak,
cut into hand-sized pieces**

2 eggs

2 cups flour

2 cups milk

1 teaspoon salt

2 tablespoons pepper

4 cups shortening or vegetable oil

Beat eggs; mix with milk in 3-inch deep round pan.
Place flour in similar pan.

Season meat with salt and pepper; place 4 to 5 pieces in milk
mixture and let stand while heating 1 1/2 to 2 inches of oil in
large iron skillet or Dutch oven. Heat oil to 350°. Dredge meat
in flour one piece at a time, back in milk, and again in flour.
Place in hot oil and cook 2 to 3 minutes per side, turning
once. Drain on paper towels.

While first batch is cooking, prepare next batch of steaks to
be double-dipped just as previous batch is removed from frying pan. Save browned bits left in oil for making Steak Gravy.

Serves 12 to 14

Pan-Fried
Steak

Cowboys like most anything fried, even
their steak on occasion. This is always a
crowd pleaser.

7 to 8 pounds round steak
3 cups flour
3 tablespoons freshly ground black pepper
3 teaspoons kosher salt
2 cups vegetable oil
3 large sliced onions

Cut fat from round steak and save. Tenderize steak with
tenderizer hammer or edge of metal plate by hammering
one way and then hammering across first cuts. Cut into hand-
sized pieces. Place fat in large skillet and render fat. Remove
and discard pieces that did not render.

Salt and pepper each piece and dredge both sides in flour.
Place several pieces at a time in a large skillet, cooking 2 to 3
minutes per side until golden brown, turning once. Place on
paper towels and then in warm Dutch oven until serving time.

Repeat process until all meat is cooked. Vegetable oil may be
used in skillet if you run out of rendered fat.

Slice onions and sauté until soft, placing a slice on each piece
of meat when serving.

Make Steak Gravy, *recipe page 60*. Put gravy on plate, steak
on gravy, topping with a slice of sautéed onion.

Serves 12 to 14

Chicken-Fried Steak

Smothered
Steak

Serve this steak with mashed potatoes, a green vegetable or green salad, and bread. It makes a hearty meal and you may use different cuts of beef.

4 **pounds round steak, sirloin tip, or clod steak, tenderized**
1 **teaspoon salt**
1 **tablespoon pepper**
6 **ounces fresh mushrooms, sliced**
1 **red bell pepper, diced**
3 **cups beef broth**
2 **cups flour**
2 **cups vegetable oil**
2 **cups sliced yellow onions**

Preheat oven to 350°.

Cut steak into hand-sized pieces, about 8 to 10 steaks. Salt and pepper meat. Dredge in flour and fry in oil over medium-high heat, about 2 minutes per side. Drain on paper towels. Place meat in medium-sized oven pan, cover with mushrooms, onion and bell pepper. Pour beef broth over mixture. Bake for 1 hour.

 Serves 8

Texas Cowboy
Reunion Sirloin

This recipe comes from Gerald Proctor, who is the host of the "The Cabin," the rustic ranch house where special guests are entertained, at the Texas Cowboy Reunion in Stamford, Texas. Held annually on or near the 4th of July, the Cowboy Reunion is the largest amateur rodeo in the world. People come from all around to visit with good friends, talk about the drought or brag about their inch of rain. A good time is had by all.

4 **pounds sirloin steaks, 1 inch thick**
6 **lemons, juiced**
garlic powder to taste
coarsely ground black pepper to taste
salt to taste

Two hours prior to grilling, coat both sides of steaks with lemon juice and seasonings. One hour prior to grilling, build a mesquite fire and burn down to coals. Shovel coals underneath grill to heat it up. Adjust grill to at least 8 inches above coals. Grill about 4 minutes on each side or to desired doneness. Medium rare is best because it leaves plenty of juice in the steak. Do not overcook.

Serves 6 to 8

Cookshack
Round

Whole rounds may weigh up to 30 pounds. Figure 1/2 pound per person for serving. Adjust seasonings accordingly. This large roast takes time, but is worth the wait. Serve with hot Sourdough Biscuits.

1 whole round, 10 to 20 pounds
olive oil to coat meat
1 cup coarsely ground black pepper
1 cup Western Wagons Beef Seasoning, *recipe follows*

Coat round with olive oil, follow with seasonings. Place meat on grill 30 inches above medium hot mesquite coals. Add coals to keep pit about 250°. This will take 6 to 8 hours to cook.

Serves 6 to 8

Western Wagons Beef Seasoning

1 cup freshly ground black pepper
2/3 cup salt
1/4 cup cayenne pepper
1/4 cup garlic powder
1 tablespoon sugar

Thoroughly mix all ingredients and rub on beef roasts or beef steaks. Store in dry container in refrigerator. Keeps for two to three weeks.

BEFORE REFRIGERATION

Clifford Teinert's grandfather belonged to a "beef club" near Copperas Cove, Texas in the days before refrigeration. Each week, ranchers in this German community would gather to butcher a calf furnished by one of the club members. The men would bring clean flour sacks and take home just enough beef to feed their families until the next week when another calf would be slaughtered.

Beef
Tips

As with many beef recipes, different cuts can be substituted with this recipe. Seasoning and cooking time are important to this dish's success. Serve over rice.

8 **pounds sirloin steak, trimmed and cut into 1-inch cubes**
4 **cups mushrooms, halved**
2 **cups diced onions**
4 **tablespoons vegetable oil**
3 **cups flour**
2 **teaspoons kosher salt or sea salt**
2 **tablespoons dried parsley**
3 **tablespoons freshly ground black pepper**
8 **cups hot water**
1 **cup red wine (Burgundy)**

Season meat with salt and pepper; dredge in flour. Heat vegetable oil in 16-inch Dutch oven. Brown meat in oil for about 10 minutes. Add mushrooms and onions and brown an additional 10 minutes. Add parsley, wine and hot water; reduce heat. Cover and simmer 2 to 2^1/$_2$ hours, stirring every 30 minutes.

Serve with Wild Texas Rice, *recipe page 139,* and Sourdough Biscuits, *recipe page 40.*

 Serves 16 to 20

Keep 'em Sharp!

Nothing thwarts a cook more than a dull knife—whether you're cutting rib eye steaks or slicing brisket to feed the masses. Clifford and Bill swear by a ceramic steel to keep their knives sharp because today's tempered steel is so hard. They suggest you watch a butcher at work…the knife will be sharpened every few cuts.

Dutch Oven
Roast

Cooked in a Dutch oven or roasting pan, accompanied by different vegetables, this pot roast is a one-pot meal. Use either a bone-in or boneless roast.

8 pound chuck roast, 2- to 3-inches thick, bone in if available

$^{1}/_{4}$ cup vegetable oil

$^{1}/_{2}$ cup Burgundy wine

2 cups warm water

3 cups sliced yellow onions

2 cloves garlic, chopped

1 teaspoon salt

2 tablespoons coarsely ground black pepper

$^{1}/_{2}$ cup mushrooms, sliced

6 carrots, cut into sticks

3 tablespoons cornstarch

$^{1}/_{2}$ cup water

If cooking in oven, preheat to 350°.

Heat vegetable oil in 16-inch Dutch oven or oven-proof roasting pan. Salt and pepper roast on both sides. Sear both sides in hot oil. Pour warm water and Burgundy wine over roast; add garlic, onions, carrots and sliced mushrooms. Cover and cook about 2$^{1}/_{2}$ hours, turning every 30 to 45 minutes.

If done in oven, cook for 2 to 2$^{1}/_{2}$ hours, turning only once. If roast becomes too dry, add hot water $^{1}/_{2}$ cup at a time.

Pour cooking liquid into a large measuring cup. Skim away fat. If necessary, add a little water or red wine to make 4 cups liquid and return to the cooking pan. Stir in the cornstarch dissolved in $^{1}/_{2}$ cup water. Bring to a boil, reduce heat and simmer for 3 minutes.

Return roast to cooking pan and arrange vegetables around the roast. Cover and allow to rest 15 minutes before serving.

Serves 14 to 16

Dutch Oven Roast

Cowboy
Hash

As with many of our recipes, this was created to use leftover roast beef—another hearty meal.

3 to 4 pounds leftover boneless roast beef, cubed
6 large potatoes, peeled and diced in small cubes
1¹/2 cups diced onion
4 tablespoons flour
2 cups water
salt and pepper
1 tablespoon oil

Preheat oven to 350°.

When dicing meat, discard any fat. Place meat and potatoes in large baking pan or dish and set aside. Sauté onion in oil until soft; stir onion into meat and potatoes. Pour enough water in pan to reach halfway mark around meat and potatoes. Sprinkle salt and pepper over mixture. Cover and bake for 45 minutes. Mix flour in cold water. Add to meat-potato mixture until gravy just begins to thicken. Place back in oven for 15 minutes. Remove and serve over biscuits or sourdough bread.

 **Serves 10 to 12**

Dutch Oven
Beef Pie

While sitting around the wagon one day, good friend Bud Lowrey told us about Jimbo Humphreys's version of this dish. Jimbo was a mighty fine chuck wagon cook—but it still took several years to perfect this recipe. Top with Pico de Gallo and you have another one-pot meal.

6 cups Camp Chili, *recipe page 71*
6 cups cooked Pinto Beans, *recipe page 131*
8 ears corn, kernels cut from cob
2 quantities of Best Basic Cornbread, *recipe page 47*

Pour prepared Camp Chili in a 16-inch Dutch oven. Spread with wooden spoon. Add cooked Pinto Beans and smooth with spoon. Cut corn from ears and layer over beans, spreading smoothly. In a mixing bowl, double cornbread recipe, and pour batter over corn.

Cover; cook over coals 25 to 30 minutes until cornbread is brown. Let rest 10 minutes and serve with Pico de Gallo, *recipe page 123*.

To cook in home kitchen, preheat oven to 375°.
Bake 25 to 30 minutes until cornbread is brown.

 **Serves 12 to 14**

Mountain
Oysters

This is the by-product of turning bulls into steers and is considered a delicacy by ranch hands and owners alike. A great appetizer.

2 pounds mountain oysters, cleaned
2 eggs
2 cups milk
1/2 cup coarsely ground black pepper
2 tablespoons salt
3 tablespoons Cavender's Greek Seasoning
2 cups flour
1 cup cornmeal

To clean mountain oysters, remove first membrane. Place in boiling water for 1 minute to loosen the meat from the skin. Cool slightly, then slice skin with sharp knife to expose or pop out the meat.

Beat together milk and eggs. Soak oysters in milk mixture, remove, then season. Coat with flour and cornmeal mixture. You may prefer flour or cornmeal alone rather than the mixture. Fry in hot oil.

 **Serves 8 to 10**

Beef
and Beans

This is good for cooking all day when you're camped out. It's a one-pot meal ready when everyone makes it back to camp.

3 pounds boneless beef roast, preferably sirloin
1 pound pinto beans
3 slices thick-sliced bacon
7 cups water
1/2 cup chopped onion
3 cloves garlic, minced
1 tablespoon kosher or sea salt
2 tablespoons chili powder
1 tablespoon cumin
1 tablespoon oregano
3 serrano peppers, chopped

Dice bacon and sauté lightly with onions in a 14-inch Dutch oven. Add remaining ingredients and bring to boil. Reduce heat, cover and cook on low heat for about 5 hours. Break up or slice meat and serve over tortillas or corn chips, topping with grated cheese, lettuce, tomatoes, guacamole and Pico de Gallo, *recipe page 123.*

 Serves 6 to 8

Clear Fork
Meatloaf

A good meatloaf is full of meat, not full of filler. Don't try to entice a cowboy to eat meatloaf that's not meaty.

2 pounds ground round
2 beaten eggs
1 cup uncooked oatmeal
2 tablespoons Worcestershire sauce
1 1/2 cups diced onion
1 10-ounce can diced tomatoes with green chiles
1 red bell pepper, diced
1 teaspoon salt
1 teaspoon freshly cracked black pepper
1/4 cup Granddad Mickan's BBQ Sauce, *recipe page 121*

Preheat oven to 350°.

Mix all ingredients except barbecue sauce or catsup. Shape into a loaf. Place in 11x16-inch baking pan. Cook 1 1/4 to 1 1/2 hours. Baste top with barbecue sauce or catsup 15 to 20 minutes before done.

 Serves 8

Don't try to entice a cowboy to eat meatloaf that's not meaty.

Clear Fork Chili con Carne

Clear Fork
Chili con Carne

All you need with this is a big slice of Jalapeño Cornbread.

4 pounds lean ground beef
(use chili grind for chunkier consistency)
2 cups chopped onion
3 cloves garlic, minced
1 teaspoon ground oregano
1 teaspoon cumin seed
2 tablespoons chili powder, rounded
1 dried red chile, coarsely chopped
3 cups water, more if needed

Sear meat in heavy iron skillet. Add onion and garlic, and cook 5 to 6 minutes, stirring frequently. Add remaining ingredients. Blend and bring to boil.

Reduce heat to low and simmer 1 hour.

 Serves 8

Camp
Chili

Chili is great for parties—whether it's cool outside or not. You can always freeze leftovers in various sized freezer bags to pop into a microwave oven for a quick meal. Coarsely chopping your own steak makes a heartier chili; you can always substitute hamburger meat.

7 to 8 pounds round steak, cut into 1-inch pieces
1 pound thick-sliced bacon, chopped
4 cups diced onions
$1/4$ cup flour
2 tablespoons kosher or sea salt
1 tablespoon freshly ground black pepper
8 cloves garlic, crushed
4 large tomatoes, chopped
2 tablespoons ground cumin
2 tablespoons paprika
8 poblano peppers, roasted, peeled and chopped (See page 138.)
4 cups beef stock

Brown bacon in large Dutch oven over medium heat. Add onions before bacon is done and continue browning until onions are soft. Dip bacon and onions out.

Dredge meat in flour, salt and pepper. Place in Dutch oven, stirring continuously until beef is browned. Return cooked bacon and onions to pan; add garlic. Stir and brown 2 to 3 minutes. Add ground cumin, paprika, peppers, tomatoes, beef stock and enough water to cover completely. Bring to a boil. Cover and simmer for $2 1/2$ hours or until tender, stirring occasionally, adding a little water as needed.

Serves 12 to 14 hungry men

Black Bean
Casserole

This one-dish meal pleases cowboys or company.

2 pounds ground beef (half ground round, half chuck)
1 cup chopped yellow onions
2 cups cooked black beans, drained
1 to 2 tablespoons chili powder
2 teaspoons ground cumin
salt to taste
4 flour tortillas
1 cup sliced mushrooms
3 tablespoons butter
3 tablespoons flour
1 cup chicken stock
1 cup milk
10-ounce can tomatoes with green chiles
1 cup shredded sharp Cheddar cheese

Preheat oven to 350°.

In skillet, cook beef and onions until done; drain. Add beans, chili powder, cumin and salt. Mix and pour into a nonstick 9 x 13-inch pan. Arrange tortillas on top.

Sauté mushrooms in butter for 2 to 3 minutes. Add flour and stir to combine. Gradually add stock and milk, whisking until smooth. Add tomatoes, stirring to blend. Pour sauce over tortillas. Sprinkle with cheese. Bake uncovered for 25 to 30 minutes until heated thoroughly. Serve hot.

 Serves 8

Dutch Oven
Stew

You will find this stew a wonderful fireside one-dish meal for cold winter evenings.

6 pounds boneless sirloin, cut into 1- to $1^{1}/_{2}$-inch cubes
8 large potatoes, peeled and cubed
4 tomatoes, chopped
or 10-ounce can of tomatoes and green chilies
8 carrots, scraped and chopped
4 zucchini squash, washed and chopped
4 celery stalks, chopped
$4^{1}/_{2}$ cups chopped onions
$^{1}/_{4}$ cup vegetable oil
1 tablespoon kosher salt or sea salt
2 tablespoons freshly ground black pepper
4 cups beef broth
4 cups hot water

Heat vegetable oil in 16-inch Dutch oven. Add meat and brown. Add onions and continue browning until onions are soft. Add hot water, beef stock, tomatoes, carrots, salt and pepper. Bring to a boil. Cover, reduce heat and simmer for 1 to $1^{1}/_{2}$ hours, stirring occasionally.

Add potatoes, celery and zucchini. Cover and cook an additional 30 to 45 minutes. Add hot water or broth as needed.

Serve steaming hot in large soup bowls with hot bread.

Serves 12 to 14

Green Chile
Stew

This stew is good with beef or pork
or a combination of the two.

6 **tablespoons olive oil**
3 **pounds beef or pork (round or chuck),**
  cut into 1-inch cubes
salt and black pepper
$1/2$ **cup flour, white or whole wheat**
$1^{1}/2$ **cups chopped onion**
3 **cloves garlic, minced**
10 **poblano or Big Jim peppers, roasted, peeled,**
  seeded and chopped
2 **cups chicken stock**
$1/2$ **teaspoon cumin**
$1/2$ **teaspoon dried oregano**
$1/4$ **cup fresh cilantro, optional**

In large cast iron skillet or Dutch oven, heat 3 tablespoons
oil over medium heat. Season meat with salt and pepper;
coat with flour. Brown the beef in the oil, cooking in small
batches. Transfer to bowl or platter. Add more oil as needed.

Heat remaining 3 tablespoons oil in skillet or Dutch oven.
Add onion, stirring often until softened. Add garlic and chiles.
Transfer $1/2$ of the mixture to blender; add 1 cup of chicken
stock and process until smooth. Return the green sauce and
beef or pork to skillet. Stir in remaining chicken stock, cumin
and oregano. Simmer over medium heat for 5 minutes.
Reduce to low and cook covered for $1^{1}/2$ hours until meat is
tender. Add water if necessary. Stir in cilantro and serve hot.

Serves 6 to 8

Green Chile Stew (top)

Dutch Oven Stew (bottom)

Beef
Stroganoff

This is a rich, wine-flavored dish. We always make enough for leftovers the next day. Mix in the rice, heat it up and serve it over toasted English muffins.

4 pounds London broil
 or sirloin (extra lean), cut in 1-inch cubes
1 cup butter
3 cups mushrooms, halved
3/4 cup diced yellow onion
1 1/2 cups golden sherry
1 1/2 cups cream sherry
1/4 cup red wine
1/2 cup water
4 tablespoons flour
3 cups sour cream
1 tablespoon freshly ground black pepper
1 teaspoon kosher salt or sea salt
1 recipe Wild Texas Rice, *recipe page 139*

Trim all fat from meat when cubing. Melt butter in large wide deep skillet or cast iron pan. Sear meat 8 to 10 minutes. Add mushrooms and onions and cook on medium-high heat for 10 minutes. Add salt and pepper to taste. Reduce heat. Add golden sherry and cream sherry. Cover and simmer for 1 1/2 hours until meat is tender. Mix 3 tablespoons of flour in 1/2 cup water and stir into mixture. Add 1 tablespoon flour in 1/4 cup red wine and stir into mixture to thicken gravy. Simmer for 5 minutes. Turn off heat and stir in sour cream. Cover and let stand 30 minutes.

Serve over piping hot mounds of Wild Texas Rice.

 **Serves 8 to 10**

Beef Tortilla
Soup

This recipe comes from Jon and Jackie Means of the Moon Ranch in Van Horn, Texas. It's excellent for a cool fall evening or anytime!

2 tablespoons corn oil
4 corn tortillas
5 cloves garlic, finely chopped
1 tablespoon cilantro, chopped
1 large can tomato purée
1 1/2 cups chopped onion
1 tablespoon cumin
2 teaspoons chili powder
2 bay leaves
2 quarts beef stock, chilled and skimmed of fat, or beef broth
salt to taste
1/4 teaspoon cayenne pepper, or more if preferred
8 ounces lean cooked beef, cubed or shredded
1 medium tomato, coarsely chopped
1 avocado, peeled, seeded and cubed
1 cup Cheddar cheese, shredded
3 corn tortillas, cut into thin strips and crisply fried

Heat oil in a large saucepan over medium heat. Sauté tortillas, garlic and cilantro over medium heat to soften tortillas. Add onion and tomato purée, bring to boil. Stir in cumin, chili powder, bay leaves and beef stock. Return to boil; reduce to simmer. Cook 15 minutes and taste; add salt and cayenne pepper to taste. Cook, stirring, 15 minutes. Add beef, tomatoes and avocado to soup bowls and pour in equal portions of soup.

Garnish with cheese and tortilla strips. Serve piping hot with hot flour tortillas.

 Serves 8

GRILLS AND IMPROVISING

The original mesquite pit used by chuck wagon cooks on the range was the Open-Fire Pit, which was simply a hole in the ground rigged with a crossbar frame above it. From the bar hung S-hooks that could hold a pot or kettle such as a Dutch oven. A flat metal grill could be laid across the hole for cooking meat. To adjust for distance from coals to meat, the chuck wagon cook would dig the hole to the desired depth. The authentic Open-Fire Pit remains a desirable grilling method.

Highly convenient Barrel Grills have come into popular use. The benefit of the Upright-Barrel Grill is that it allows the cook to grill meats 24 to 30 inches from coals. With its cover and greater depth, the Upright-Barrel Grill allows the burning coals to impart their smoke flavor to the meat. The versatile Split-Barrel Grill, with its horizontal orientation, has a greater surface area, allowing the cook to use indirect heat for smoking at one end while using high, direct heat for grilling steaks on the other end. Coals lie at a distance of 10 to 12 inches from the meat.

The Kettle Grill is a common backyard grill that can be purchased at hardware, discount and department stores. It allows meat to be grilled 4 to 10 inches from the coals.

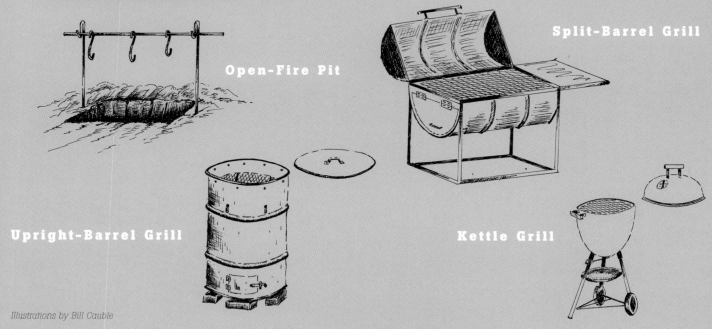

Open-Fire Pit

Split-Barrel Grill

Upright-Barrel Grill

Kettle Grill

Illustrations by Bill Cauble

Crown Roast of Lamb

Crown Roast
of Lamb

A dramatic roast for special occasions!

3 3-pound racks of lamb
1 1/2 cups water
1 cup white wine
1 small onion, coarsely chopped
8 cloves garlic,
several sprigs of fresh rosemary

Stand the racks, rib ends up, ends together to form a circle. Form the circle around an empty 24-ounce tin can. Lace the ends together using butcher twine.

Moisten the surface of the meat and the exposed bones with olive oil. Season well with Spice Rub for Lamb, Venison and Cabrito, *recipe page 78*. Fill the can with the water, wine, onion and garlic. Roast on the grill, 24 inches above mesquite coals, until an internal temperature of 160° is reached, for medium doneness.

In the home kitchen, preheat oven to 375°. Roast approximately 40 minutes, until an internal temperature of 160° is reached, for medium doneness.

When done, remove the can and discard the contents, and place roast on a large platter. Fill center with roasted potatoes, or Wild Texas Rice, *recipe page 139*, and sprigs of fresh rosemary. Carve between ribs to serve.

 Serves 8

Rack of
Lamb

Spice Rub for Lamb, Venison and Cabrito

2 tablespoons coarsely ground pepeper
1 teaspoon cumin
1 teaspoon ground cayenne pepper
2 cloves garlic, finely minced
1 tablespoons rosemary leaves, chopped

Combine and rub onto oiled meat. Allow meat to rest with rub on for a few minutes before cooking.

Slow grilling makes the meat more tender.

1 3- to 4-pound rack of lamb
1/2 cup olive oil
2 tablespoons balsamic vinegar
1 teaspoon salt
2 tablespoons coarsely ground black pepper
1 teaspoon ground cumin
1/2 teaspoon cayenne pepper
2 cloves garlic, crushed

Coat rack of lamb with oil and spices that have been mixed together. Place on grill, bone side down, about 18 inches above mesquite coals. Grill for about 20 minutes, turn and cook on meat side for 30 minutes. Continue turning and basting with oil and spices until done, about 170°.

We also grill the rack of lamb on the "steak grill" setting, 6 to 8 inches from hot coals, for approximately 5 minutes on each side. Watch carefully to avoid over cooking. We like these chops medium done…pink centered…with an internal temperature of 160°. Baste several times during cooking.

Serves 4

Chicken-Fried
Venison Strips

This is an excellent appetizer or main course.

2 pounds venison round, cut into finger-sized strips
2 cups buttermilk or milk
2 cups sliced yellow onions
$1/2$ cup coarsely ground black pepper
2 tablespoons salt
1 teaspoon ground red pepper
1 tablespoon garlic powder
1 cup flour

Soak venison strips in milk for at least two hours. Combine spices with flour. Remove venison strips from milk and coat with flour mixture. Fry in 1 inch of hot oil. Place onion slices on top of meat as you fry. Drain on paper towels.

 Serves 6

Chicken-Fried Venison Strips

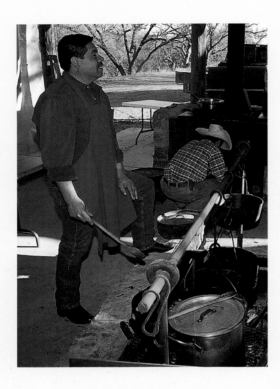

Venison
Backstrap

While cooking a whole backstrap and some bacon-wrapped venison tenderloin steaks one evening, friend Don Koch suggested using orange slices atop the venison to prevent dryness. It works every time.

1 venison backstrap
6 slices bacon
6 thick slices of orange, peel on
Brisket Rub, *recipe page 59*
6 toothpicks

Rub all sides of backstrap with Brisket Rub. Wrap outside edges with bacon; secure with toothpick. Place on grill over medium-hot coals. Place orange slices on venison. Cook 15 minutes per side, removing and replacing orange slices until meat begins to firm and internal temperature of 150° is reached for medium doneness.

To cook in home kitchen, preheat oven to 350°.

Follow instructions for coating meat with Brisket Rub. Roast for approximately 30 minutes until internal temperature reaches 150° for medium. Remove from oven and let meat rest for 10 minutes before carving.

TIP: The backstrap is the venison tenderloin.

Serve hot.

 Serves 6

Venison
Leg

The secret to venison is to cook it slowly, basting often.

1 **leg of venison**
3 to 4 **cups water**
1 **cup vinegar**
2 **tablespoons salt**
2 **tablespoons freshly ground black pepper**
3 **lemons, sliced**
1 **cup olive or vegetable oil**

Combine water, oil and seasoning. Boil for 5 minutes. Pour over venison. Cover and let stand in the marinade overnight. Keep cool.

Place on grill about 30 inches from mesquite coals. Reheat the marinade and use to baste the venison, adding more liquid if needed. Turn the meat every hour. About one hour before meat is done, wrap in heavy foil and continue cooking. This will help tenderize the meat. Allow 2 to 3 hours cooking time.

To cook in home kitchen, preheat oven to 350°.

Follow instructions for marinating meat. Roast for approximately 20 minutes per pound, basting frequently with marinade, until internal temperature reaches 150° for medium or 160° for medium well doneness. Remove from oven and let meat rest for 10 minutes before carving.

Serves 8

Venison Leg *(top)*

Venison Backstrap *(bottom)*

Clockwise from top left:
mesquite in spring foliage with
Texas bluebonnets; mesquite
wood pile; mesquite wood fire—
coals in the making; cooking
briskets over mesquite coals;
chuck-wagon cooking over a
pit of mesquite coals

WHERE BARBECUE BEGINS...
Cooking over Mesquite Coals

When cooking with wood originated is unclear—but we know wood was the only available fuel and heat source for eons. The French called cooking with wood *barbe et queue,* or cooking meat from the *barbe,* or whiskers, to the *queue,* or tail. In the early days, the whole animal was cooked at once, thus "*barbe*" to "*queue.*" There is an ongoing debate about the benefits, attributes and best methods of cooking with wood. Of course, it helps that our part of Texas is overrun with the lowly mesquite that saps rangeland of precious water. Mesquite is the bane of many a Texas rancher, but a boon for those who like to cook.

There is no debate in our minds. It's mesquite or nothing.

Correctly used, mesquite has no peer for heat capacity, flavor enhancement, handling ease and temperature control. Slow-cooked over mesquite coals, less tender meat cuts become a gourmet's delight. We point you to the brisket to illustrate this. Once known as one of the sorriest pieces of meat on the animal, brisket prepared over a bed of mesquite coals is a culinary delight. Of course, the key ingredients are patience and proper use of the wood.

The best mesquite for cooking has been on the ground for 8 months to a year—aged and well-seasoned.

The "greenness," or acrid flavor, disappears after this aging process, resulting in an unmatched-by-other-woods flavor. Freshly-cut mesquite has a 48 percent water content that prevents it from burning down to good coals. Mesquite is much denser than other popular cooking woods like hickory, pecan or oak.

The proof is in the coals.

Meat should be cooked over mesquite coals that have burned down to a red-white glow in the hard part of the coals. These hard coals hold heat and release flavor, in the form of smoke, over a long period of time.

For fast grilling of steaks, chops, chicken and other small pieces of meat, the grill should be 6 to 8 inches above the coals.

For slow cooking of whole rib eyes, large rounds, whole pigs, briskets, whole chickens or turkeys and other large pieces of meat, the grill should be 24 to 30 inches above the coals.

Briskets should be cooked for 10 to 12 hours over coals producing steady heat of about 212°, the boiling point of water. Meats should be cooked fat side up so that nature and gravity do the basting. However, we like to use our Barbecue Mop Sauce, *recipe page 121*, to keep leaner meats moist.

The Good Lord has provided the meat and mesquite. All you have to do is enjoy the cooking and the eating.

CHICKEN & GAME BIRDS

Never put barbecue sauce on your meat until the very last.
This will keep your grill cleaner and the sauce tastier.

Mesquite-Grilled
Chicken

When grilling chicken, place the grill at least 18 inches above the coals to ensure even cooking. The slower it cooks, the better it is. Never put barbecue sauce on your meat until the very last. This will keep your grill cleaner and the sauce tastier.

2 chickens, halved and well rinsed

MARINADE	
1 cup vinegar	1 tablespoon chili powder
1 cup water	1 tablespoon black pepper
1/2 cup olive oil	1 tablespoon salt
1 teaspoon ground cumin	1 clove garlic, chopped
	1 cup diced onion

Place chickens in glass or stainless steel bowl.

Combine marinade ingredients in stainless saucepan and bring to boil. Simmer 15 to 20 minutes. Pour marinade over chickens. Cover with plastic wrap and refrigerate overnight.

Place chicken on grill, skin side down to keep the juice in, over low mesquite coals. Turn the halves with a rag or tongs only after the skin is really browned. Do not use a fork because the juices will run out. Cook until leg bone starts to slip out of the meat. Place on platter and cover with Granddad Mickan's BBQ Sauce, *recipe page 121.*

TIP: If you are presssed for time, these chickens may be grilled at the "steak grill setting" with the grill 6 to 8 inches above the coals. But you must watch carefully to keep from burning, and turn and baste frequently.

Serves 6 to 8

Marinated
Chicken Breasts

Even people who say they don't like chicken breasts like this dish. It's always a favorite.

8 8-ounce skinless, boneless chicken breasts
2 cups sliced yellow onions
2 cloves garlic, pressed
1 red bell pepper, thinly sliced
2 jalapeños, diced
1 teaspoon ground cayenne pepper, divided
1 recipe Brisket Rub, *recipe page 59,* **with no black pepper**
olive oil

Pour a thin layer of olive oil on bottom of container with tight-fitting lid. Flatten 4 chicken breasts out on oil. Sprinkle with rub and 1/2 teaspoon cayenne pepper. Layer with half of the onions, bell pepper, garlic and jalapeño. Repeat with remaining chicken breasts, seasoning and vegetables. Just cover with olive oil. Refrigerate overnight. Remove and cook on grill, 6 to 8 inches above hot coals, 4 to 6 minutes per side.

Serves 8

Jalapeño Pepper

Oven-Baked
Chicken Halves

The halves can be quartered after cooking by taking tongs and sliding under thigh to remove it and drumstick.

3 whole fryers, halved and washed
3 lemons, halved
1 teaspoon rosemary, chopped
1 teaspoon thyme, crushed
2 tablespoons freshly ground black pepper
1 teaspoon salt
$1^1/2$ cups water

Preheat oven to 350°.

Pour water into a 12 x 18-inch pan or two smaller pans. Place chickens, cut side down, into pan; squeeze ½ lemon over each half, discarding seeds. Mix all dry seasoning ingredients. Rub each chicken half with seasonings. Cover and bake 1 hour 45 minutes. Uncover and bake an additional 15 to 20 minutes. Remove and serve.

 **Serves 6 or 12**

Bacon-Wrapped
Chicken Livers

We grilled 500 of these for a Christmas party once. They take a lot more time to prepare than to eat, but they're worth the extra work. They're also good as a main dish.

9 slices bacon, halved
18 chicken livers
18 water chestnuts, whole
3 cups vegetable oil

Cut bacon slices in half. Fold chicken liver around water chestnut and wrap with bacon, securing with toothpick. Heat vegetable oil to 350 to 375°. Drop livers in oil and deep fry for about 4 to 5 minutes. Remove and drain on paper towel. Place on low-to-medium-hot pit with lots of smoke. Smoke for 20 to 25 minutes.

Serve hot or cold.

 **Serves 5 to 6**

Chicken
and Dumplings

This dish has long been a Sunday dinner favorite in Texas and the South. It's also a good way to use leftover chicken.

1 **whole chicken, 3 to 4 pounds**
4 **cups chicken stock**
3 **cups flour**
1 **teaspoon salt**
$^1/_2$ **cup butter**
1 **teaspoon pepper**

Boil whole or cut-up chicken with giblets in water to cover until tender, 30 to 35 minutes. Remove chicken skin and bones; reserving stock. Chop chicken into 1-inch pieces and set aside; giblets can be chopped if desired. Strain stock into 20-inch stock pot. Add chicken, butter, pepper and chicken stock. Heat to boil.

Combine flour and salt in mixing bowl. Add just enough cold water to make a ball. Roll out on a well-floured cutting board until dough is $^1/_4$-inch thick. Cut into long, 1- to $1^1/_2$-inch wide strips; cut those strips into 3- to 4-inch pieces. Cut all dumplings at once; place on generously floured cookie sheet even if you have to stack dumplings. Place dumplings individually into boiling broth. It's fine if they stack up. Cover and cook 5 minutes. Add chopped chicken. Remove from heat, stir and serve.

TIP: Well-floured dumplings will thicken the broth.

 Serves 8 to 10

Winter Squash Stuffed **with Chicken**

This, with a green salad, is a complete meal.

6 winter squash (acorn or butternut)
4 8-ounce skinless, boneless chicken breasts
4 cups water
1 teaspoon salt
2 ears of corn, kernels removed
1 red bell pepper, diced
1 cup diced yellow onions
1 jalapeño, diced
1/2 cup butter
salt and pepper

Preheat oven to 350°.

Cut top off squash and remove seeds. Place cut side down in 1/2 inch of water in baking pan. Bake 45 to 50 minutes until squash is tender. While squash is baking, prepare stuffing.

STUFFING: Cook chicken breasts in salted water to cover until done, about 20 minutes; dice. Melt butter in medium pan. Add corn and onions and sauté 10 minutes. Add chicken, bell pepper and jalapeño. Cook over low heat 2 to 3 minutes. Add salt and pepper to taste.

Dry inside of squash with paper towel. Add stuffing and bake, stuffing side up, in same pan without water for 10 minutes.

Serve hot.

 Serves 6

Chicken **Casserole**

This recipe can also be made with leftover chicken or turkey.

4 8-ounce boneless, skinless chicken breasts
4 stalks celery, diced
1 cup diced onion
2 cloves garlic, pressed
11/2 cups mushrooms, sliced
1/2 cup butter
1/2 cup wild rice, uncooked
1 cup long grain rice, uncooked
4 tablespoons flour
4 cups chicken stock
1 tablespoon dried parsley
1 teaspoon kosher salt
1 teaspoon freshly ground black pepper

Preheat oven to 350°.

Boil chicken breasts in water until tender, about 20 to 25 minutes. Remove and chop into 1/2-inch cubes. While chicken breasts are cooking, sauté celery, onions, mushrooms and pressed garlic in pan with butter until onions are tender, about 10 to 15 minutes. Put cooked ingredients in 9 x 13-inch baking dish or deep 14-inch cake pan. Stir in rice, flour and chicken stock. Add parsley, salt and pepper. Bake for 60 to 70 minutes.

 Serves 8

Stacked Red Chile Enchiladas

Stacked Red Chile
Enchiladas

In New Mexico, the enchiladas are stacked rather than rolled. We order red chile ristras from New Mexico to make our own red chile sauce—you can taste the difference.

West Texas Basic Red Chile Sauce, *recipe page 120*
1 pound sharp Cheddar cheese, grated
1 large onion, chopped
2 dozen corn tortillas
1 cup olive oil or vegetable oil
8 eggs

In heavy skillet, heat oil. Quickly dip tortillas into hot oil until softened but not tough. Place one tortilla flat on oven-safe serving plate, add chile sauce to cover, then sprinkle with cheese and onions. Repeat twice. Place plate in hot oven to melt cheese. Top each stack with a fried egg. Serve immediately with a green salad and an ice-cold beer.

 Serves 8

Green Chile Enchiladas
with Chicken

This dish is influenced by West Texas ranchers, who borrow heavily from their New Mexico neighbors.

1 cup chopped onion
2 cloves garlic, chopped
2 cups green chiles, poblanos or Anaheims, roasted, peeled and chopped
2 tomatoes, peeled and chopped
1/2 teaspoon salt
1/2 teaspoon oregano
1/2 teaspoon pepper
1/2 teaspoon ground cumin
3 tablespoons butter
3 tablespoons flour
1/2 cup chicken stock
1 cup milk
1 cup sour cream
1 cup cooked chicken, diced
1 dozen corn tortillas
2 cups grated Longhorn cheese
oil

Preheat oven to 325°.

Brown onion and garlic in heavy skillet; add chopped chiles and tomatoes. Combine all spices, mix into chile mixture and simmer 15 minutes. Meanwhile, cook butter and flour together for 2 to 3 minutes. Over medium heat, stirring constantly, gradually add stock and milk. Continue to simmer for 3 minutes, as sauce thickens, whisking to keep smooth. Remove from heat. Stir in sour cream; add chicken.

Heat oil. Dip tortillas into hot oil until softened but not tough. Drain on paper towels.

In nonstick baking dish, alternate layers of tortillas, green chile mixture, chicken mixture and cheese. Top with cheese and bake 20 minutes.

 Serves 6

Chicken, Pasta and
Green Chile Chowder

This is great if you have leftover chicken. Green chile is a favorite complement to poultry.

4 tablespoons olive oil
2 cloves garlic, minced
1 1/2 cups chopped onion
4 chicken breasts or 6 thighs, boned and diced
1 red bell pepper, chopped
3 green chiles, roasted, peeled and chopped
6 cups chicken broth
1 pound fresh pasta
1 tablespoon freshly ground black pepper
1 1/2 quarts water
1 cup milk or half-and-half

In large heavy pot, heat oil. Add onion and chicken; cook until browned. Add pepper and chiles, simmer until tender. Add milk, broth and water, bring to a boil. Add pasta and simmer 5 minutes or until pasta is tender. Season with black pepper and salt to taste.

Serve in large soup bowls.

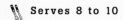 **Serves 8 to 10**

Green Chile

Garland's
Texas Gumbo

When making the roux, it must reach a deep rich brown color—but keep stirring. It'll be ready then.

2 small chickens or a combination of duck, dove or quail
2 gallons water, plus a little
3 cups chopped onions
2 large green bell peppers, chopped
5 cloves garlic, chopped
1 cup oil
1 cup flour
2 cups chopped green onions
2 pounds sliced okra
salt, black pepper, red pepper to taste
2 pounds shrimp, cooked, peeled and chopped
1 pound crabmeat, picked over for shell
2 tablespoons gumbo filé powder

Boil chickens or game birds in large pot; reserve broth. De-bone and cut into bite-sized pieces. Return to broth; add next three ingredients and simmer over medium heat for 30 minutes. Add salt and pepper to taste.

Pour oil into hot cast iron skillet. When oil is hot, stir in flour to form a paste and cook, stirring constantly with a wire whisk, until the roux is a rich nutty brown. Add green onions. Whisking constantly, gradually add three cups broth to the roux. Then pour the roux into the remaining broth, whisking until smooth.

Add okra 15 minutes before serving. Add shrimp, crabmeat and gumbo filé 10 minutes before serving.

Serve over a scoop of white rice in large soup bowls. Be sure to equalize the seafood "goodies" when divvying up the gumbo.

 Serves 15

Watt's
Chicken Soup

This deliciously simple soup was Watt Matthews's favorite.

4 8-ounce boneless, skinless chicken breasts
1 celery heart, about 4 small stalks
1 cup long grain rice, uncooked
4 cups chicken stock
1/2 cup diced onion
1 teaspoon pepper
1/2 teaspoon salt

Boil chicken breasts until done, about 25 to 30 minutes. Remove breasts and cut into 1/2-inch cubes. Put diced chicken in chicken stock. Bring to boil and reduce heat to simmer.

Add diced onion, chopped celery, rice, salt and pepper. Simmer for about 1 hour.

Serve with hard toasted bread or crackers.

 Serves 8 to 10

Watt's Chicken Soup

Dutch Oven
Game Hens

This is another dish in which quail can be substituted.

4 **game hens**
1½ **cups chopped yellow onions**
1 **fresh pineapple, chopped**
1 **cup golden raisins**
2 **cups pineapple juice**
½ **cup apple cider vinegar**
2 **cups chicken stock**
½ **cup butter**
3 **tablespoons flour**

Wash birds. Brown whole birds on medium hot grill or in a nonstick skillet for 15 to 20 minutes, turning once.

Melt butter in 16-inch Dutch oven. Sauté onions until soft; add fresh pineapple, golden raisins, pineapple juice and vinegar. Simmer 5 to 10 minutes. Add birds, breast up. Cover and cook slowly 25 to 30 minutes. Add chicken stock and simmer additional 45 minutes. Remove birds and keep warm. Mix flour with remains to make gravy. Dissolve the flour in 1 cup cold water, then stir into simmering chicken stock mixture. Simmer 5 minutes. Serve hot gravy with the birds.

 Serves 4 to 8

Tart Honeyed
Game Hens

Cornish hens or quail can be used in this tasty dish.

6 **game hens**
2 **quantities Tart Honeyed Sauce,** *recipe page 119*

Wash game birds in cold water. Brown back sides only over medium-hot coals with lots of smoke for 15 to 20 minutes. Place in 12 x 18-inch baking pan. Pour Tart Honeyed Sauce over hens. Maintain a gentle simmer. Turn hens after 30 minutes; repeat again on back. As sauce begins to thicken, baste continuously with basting brush, breast side up. Remove from heat before sauce becomes dark brown or too thick, approximately 2 hours.

In the home kitchen, preheat oven to 325°.

Place hens in large baking pan. Pour Tart Honeyed Sauce over hens. Bake approximately 2 hours, basting occasionally.

Serve hot with Wild Texas Rice, *recipe page 139* or Homemade Egg Noodles, *recipe page 140* and a green salad.

Serves 6 hungry men or
12 persons if hens are halved

Baked Dove
in Gravy

Labor Day attracts many dove hunters to our area. This recipe was prompted by an abundance of doves—it's a hearty meal.

12 whole doves, cleaned and split
1 teaspoon salt
1 tablespoon freshly ground black pepper
8 ounces mushrooms, finely chopped
1 cup finely chopped onion
3 cups flour
3 cups milk
3 cups chicken broth
2 cups vegetable oil

Preheat oven to 350°.

Add salt and pepper to flour in 9 x 13-inch pan. Pour milk in another pan large enough to hold 3 or 4 birds. Place birds in milk for 5 to 6 minutes. Remove and dredge in flour. Fry in cast iron skillet on medium heat for 2 to 3 minutes per side, turning once. Drain on paper towels. While first birds are cooking, soak next batch of birds. When all are cooked, pour chicken broth in 12 x 18-inch baking pan or two 9 x 13-inch Pyrex baking dishes; add mushrooms and onions. Place birds, split side down, in pan. Cover and bake 30 minutes. Uncover and bake 15 minutes. If gravy is too thick, add a little water or broth.

 Serves 6

Grilled
Wild Turkey

Our part of Texas is blessed with flocks of wild turkeys that roam the banks of the Clear Fork of the Brazos River. We know it's best if the turkey's feathers are plucked immediately after killed. Leave the "beard" attached during cooking, when possible, for drama—not for eating.

1 **wild turkey, plucked and cleaned**	$^1/_2$ **cup salt**
1 **gallon water, or enough to cover**	$^1/_2$ **cup vinegar**

Mix water, salt and vinegar in large pan with cover. Cover turkey with mixture and let stand overnight.

Before cooking, stuff the body and neck cavities with your choice of sliced fruit, celery, onions and parsley for a moist and more flavorful bird.

SAUCE

$^1/_2$ **cup butter**	1 **lemon, sliced**
2 **cups water**	1 **cup diced onions**
1 **cup vinegar**	2 **cloves garlic, diced**
2 **tablespoons black pepper**	1 **tablespoon chili powder**

Combine all ingredients in medium saucepan; boil for 30 minutes. Place turkey about 22 to 30 inches above coals, basting every 30 minutes. Cook very slowly for about 4 to 5 hours until internal temperature reaches 175 to 180°.

In the home kitchen, preheat oven to 350°.

Roast, basting frequently, 15 minutes per pound until internal temperature reaches 180°.

 Serves 2 to 3 persons per pound

Grilled Wild Turkey

PORK

★

Your mesquite coals should be hot, but not as hot as for beef steaks.

Fresh Pork Ham
on the Pit

Watt Matthews liked to give these as Christmas gifts—the West Texas answer to Southern smoked hams.

1 5-pound ham
olive oil

SEASONING
1/4 cup coarsely ground black pepper
2 tablespoons chili powder
1 teaspoon cayenne pepper
1 tablespoon cumin
2 tablespoons salt
olive oil or vegetable oil
Granddad Mickan's Barbecue Sauce, *recipe page 121*

Mix all seasonings in bowl. Recipe is enough for a 5-pound roast or ham.

Three to four hours prior to cooking or overnight, coat fresh ham with olive oil and seasoning. Place on pit, at least 28 to 30 inches above mesquite coals. Cook slowly for 4 to 5 hours. Internal ham temperature should be 170° when done.

Top with Granddad Mickan's Barbecue Sauce.

 Serves 8

Baby Back Pork Ribs
with **Tart Honeyed Sauce**

Baby back ribs are those that have the cartilage and excess fat removed by the butcher. They are easy to handle and serve. The butcher will charge more, but there is less waste.

2 sides baby back pork ribs, approximately 4 pounds each
4 recipes Tart Honeyed Sauce, *recipe page 119*
4 tablespoons Brisket Rub, *recipe page 59*

Rub both sides of ribs with Brisket Rub. Brown on both sides over medium to hot coals in a covered pit or covered cooker—with lots of smoke—about 30 to 35 minutes. Place ribs in a large roasting pan at least 12 x 20 inches. Pour Tart Honeyed Sauce over ribs. To maintain a gentle simmering of sauce, add coals as needed. Turn ribs every 20 to 25 minutes, basting generously with sauce. As sauce thickens, about 1 1/2 to 1 3/4 hours, you will need to continuously baste the ribs. Remove from heat before sauce turns too dark and too thick to baste. Place on serving dish or cutting board. Slice ribs individually and serve hot.

Total time—about 3 hours.

Serves 4 to 6

Roasted
Suckling Pig

The finished product is a striking addition to any table or buffet. Be sure to call a butcher well in advance to order. In our ranch country, the feral pigs are hunted with rifles—or on horseback with lassos.

15- to 25- pound suckling pig, scalded and scraped
1 red apple, peppers, onions, oranges, herbs and greenery for garnish and presentation
1 small empty coffee can
aluminum foil

After pig has been cleaned, insert a stick into the pig's mouth to prop jaws open. Place the coffee can in the body cavity to support pig during cooking. Cover ears with foil to prevent them from getting too crisp. Fold the pig's feet under the belly and tie with cotton string. Place pig on a covered grill that is about 28 to 30 inches above the coals to allow for more even heat. Add mesquite coals every 30 to 40 minutes. Oven temperature should be 250 to 300°. After one hour of cooking, remove string. It will take about 4 to 5 hours to cook. Pig should be about 170° on a meat thermometer inserted in the shoulder or ham when done. When pig is done, wipe the golden brown skin with a little oil.

To serve, place pig on large serving tray, insert an apple or large pepper into pig's mouth and place fruit and greenery—lettuce, parsley, cilantro, peppers, grapes, orange slices—around the pig. Slice through skin down middle of back and around neck. Carve and serve immediately.

Serves 15 to 20

Stuffed
Pork Loin

Buy butcher's twine in specialty grocery stores or hardware stores.

4 cups fresh spinach, washed and dried
2 tart green apples, peeled, cored and diced
1 cup golden raisins
2 tablespoons olive oil
1 whole pork loin, 6 to 7 pounds
1/4 cup freshly cracked black pepper
butcher's twine

Sauté spinach, apple and raisins in olive oil over medium heat for 7 to 10 minutes in large skillet.

Cut loin lengthwise on lean side, leaving 3/4 to 1 inch uncut. Stuff with spinach, apple and raisin mixture. Tie with string on each end, then every 3 to 4 inches. Roll in cracked pepper. Place 8 to 10 inches above medium hot coals and cook until pork reaches 160°, about 1 1/4 to 1 1/2 hours. Remove from pit and place on cutting board. Remove strings and slice 1/2 to 3/4 inch thick.

To cook in home kitchen, preheat oven to 350°.

Follow instructions for stuffing loin. Roast for 1 1/4 to 1 1/2 hours until internal temperature reaches 160˚. Remove from oven and let meat rest for 10 minutes before carving.

Serves 16 to 18

Pork Chops
and Pears

Any fruit complements pork. This is a pleasant variation.

4 pork chops, 3/4 inch thick
1 cup milk
coarsely ground black pepper, to taste
salt, to taste
Cholula hot sauce, to taste
1/2 cup olive oil
1/2 cup whole wheat flour
1/4 cup wheat germ
1 cup chopped onion
1 fresh jalapeño or serrano pepper, chopped
2 cloves garlic, chopped
1 tablespoon flour
2 large pears, sliced rounds

SAUCE	1/2 cup white wine
1/2 cup milk	1/2 cup water

Soak pork chops in 1 cup of milk for 15 minutes. Season chops with salt, pepper and hot sauce. Heat olive oil in large skillet. Combine wheat flour and germ; coat chops in flour mixture. Brown chops and remove from skillet.

Add onions and peppers to skillet and sauté. Add a little more oil if needed. Add garlic, 1 tablespoon flour and brown. Gradually add sauce mixture, stirring as it thickens.

Place pork chops back in skillet, cover and simmer for 30 minutes. Add sliced pears 10 minutes before serving.

Serve over steaming hot brown rice.

Serves 4

Grilled
Pork Chops

These are quick and easy and tasty. Your mesquite coals should be hot, but not as hot as for beef steaks. Set the grill 6 to 8 inches above the coals.

6 center-cut pork chops, 1 to 1¹/4 inches thick
1/4 cup Western Wagons Beef Seasoning, *recipe page 63*
1/4 teaspoon chopped rosemary or sage

Add the chopped rosemary or sage to the Western Wagon Beef Seasoning recipe, combine. Rub generously on both sides of chops. Grill chops over coals about 12 to 15 minutes per side. Turn more than once if the coals are extremely hot. Grill to golden brown and remove, keeping warm. Let stand 15 to 20 minutes before serving.

Serves 6

Jalapeño Peppers

Serrano Chiles

Smothered
Pork Liver

Although this recipe works well with beef liver, fresh pork liver is mild and sweet—and a great way to get iron in your diet.

3 **to 4 pounds fresh pork liver**
2 **cups sliced yellow onions**
3 **cups vegetable oil**
3 **cups flour**
$^1/_2$ **cup mushrooms, sliced**
1 **tablespoon freshly ground black pepper**
1 **teaspoon salt**
hot water

Preheat oven to 350°.

Remove the skin and membrane from pork liver. Cut liver in $^1/_3$- to $^1/_2$-inch slices. Dredge in flour seasoned with salt and pepper. Place in cast iron skillet and cook in hot oil 2 to 3 minutes per side.

Place in oven-safe pan or dish. Cover with onion and mushrooms. Add enough hot water to cover. Bake for 55 to 60 minutes.

 Serves 8

Pork Tenderloin
with **Tart Honeyed Sauce**

You can't hurry this dish, but you can slow the cooking down by adding a cup of pineapple juice to the sauce as it cooks.

4 pork tenderloins (generally two to a package)
2 recipes Tart Honeyed Sauce, *recipe page 119*
2 tablespoons Brisket Rub, *recipe page 59*

Rub tenderloins with Brisket Rub. Brown over medium hot coals for 20 to 25 minutes, rolling often to brown all sides. Place in large roasting pan at least 12 x 18 inches or two smaller pans. Pour Tart Honeyed Sauce over tenderloin. To maintain a gentle simmering of sauce, add coals as needed. Turn tenderloins every 15 to 20 minutes and baste generously with a brush. As sauce begins to thicken, continuously baste and turn tenderloins. Sauce will continue to thicken. Remove from heat before sauce blackens.

Remove tenderloins from pan and place on cutting board or serving platter. Slice 1/2 inch thick, surround with colorful sautéed sweet peppers and serve hot.

TIP: Total cooking time will be 2 to 2 1/2 hours.

To cook in home kitchen, preheat oven to 400°.

Follow instructions for preparing loin. Place in large roasting pan. Roast for 10 minutes at 400°, turning after 5 minutes. Reduce oven heat to 250°. Pour sauce over meat. Return to oven and roast for 1 hour until internal temperature reaches 160°, turning every 15 minutes. Carve and serve hot, garnished with sautéed sweet peppers.

 Serves 8

Pork Tenderloin with Tart Honeyed Sauce

FANDANGLE

Each June, the citizens of Albany, Texas, stage an historical musical production filled with drama, song and dance in an open-air prairie theater. It's a recounting of the area's settling—a story of the people and the events that shaped the West. The annual show is the culmination of hours of practice and the historical tradition captured by many of Albany's settlers over the years. It draws 10,000 visitors over six nights, and although it features amateurs, the organizers and performers are regarded as professionals.

Clifford Teinert began performing in 1964. An excellent horseman, he is a flagbearer in the high-speed, horseback flag parade which opens the show. He is a leading soloist serenading the longhorn cattle drive across the prairie stage. Bill Cauble began assisting the show's director, James Ball, in 1969. Today he serves as president of the Fandangle Association, the group that guides the production each year, and Bill's Western Wagons serves the barbecue supper on the courthouse lawn before all the Fandangle performances.

It is fitting that in Albany, Teinert and Cauble are involved in the Fandangle, the telling of the West Texas region's story featuring Indians, cowboys, soldiers, buffalo hunters, ranchers, rattlesnakes, longhorn cattle, saloons and frontier forts. The story captures the fun and the fear, and might stretch the truth a little—just for effect. In essence, it was the same for cowboys sitting around a chuck wagon fire, telling tales and singing along with a guitar or harmonica.

SOB Stew or
Gentleman from Odessa

Anywhere else a gentleman from Odessa would be called an SOB. This recipe was awarded second place at the first (and only) SOB Cookoff held at the meteor crater outside Odessa, Texas. Frank X. Tolbert, who founded the world-famous chili cookoff in Terlingua, was the judge.

one suckling calf
1¹/2 cups onion, chopped in ¹/2-inch pieces
3 cloves garlic, minced
kosher salt or sea salt and freshly ground
    black pepper, to taste

From a suckling calf, take the tongue, sweet breads, marrow, guts, ¹/4 of the liver, 1 heart, 1 kidney, skirt steaks and brains. Boil the tongue to remove outer skin. Chop all meat (except brains) into ¹/2-inch cubes.

In a 16-inch deep cast iron pot, cover ingredients with 2 inches of water and simmer for 2 hours until tender. Add or remove water as needed.

Add brains 15 minutes before serving.

Serve with Sourdough Biscuits, *recipe page 40.*

 Serves 12

Green Chile Sausage
and Potato Caldo

1 pound lean sausage
1¹/2 cups chopped onion
6 green chiles, roasted, peeled, seeded and chopped
3 garlic cloves, diced
2 pounds new potatoes, diced
4 cups chicken broth
6 cups milk
1 teaspoon salt
1 tablespoon coarsely ground black pepper

In a 14-inch Dutch oven or large skillet, brown sausage breaking it up as it cooks. Add onions and cook until soft. Add chiles, garlic, potatoes and chicken broth. Bring to boil, reduce heat and simmer for 30 minutes. Add milk, salt and black pepper, heating slowly until hot.

Serve in large bowls with hot bread.

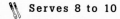 **Serves 8 to 10**

Green Chiles

Chile
Colorado

Chile Colorado

This is the way it's made in Far West Texas.
Many thanks to Frank Escobedo, longtime
friend and faithful employee of the Long X
Ranch.

5 pounds fresh pork backbones
2 quarts water
2 cups chopped yellow onions
2 to 4 garlic cloves, minced
2 tablespoons freshly ground black pepper
1 tablespoon salt
4 cups West Texas Basic Red Chile Sauce, *recipe page 120*
flour to thicken, if needed

Place pork in stock pot; add water to cover all. Add onions,
garlic, pepper and salt. Boil for 30 to 40 minutes. Cover and
simmer for 30 minutes. Pour off half of the cooking water,
reserving to add back if needed. Add chile sauce; simmer 1
hour.

Serve with pinto beans and rice.

Serves 4 to 6

FISH & MEATLESS DISHES

You're just as likely to get invited to a fish fry in Texas
as you are a barbecue.

Clear Fork
Fish Fry

You're just as likely to get invited to a fish fry in Texas as you are a barbecue. With myriad rivers, creeks, lakes and stock tanks brimming with fish, fresh fish is a favorite. Too, when trail drives crossed bodies of water, fish made a welcome change from the daily biscuits-and-beans diet the cowboys were accustomed to.

6 catfish fillets
$1/4$ cup all-purpose flour
canola oil
2 egg whites, slightly beaten
2 tablespoons milk
1 teaspoon salt
1 teaspoon fresh ground black pepper
$1/2$ teaspoon cayenne pepper
1 cup cornmeal
lemon slices

Pat fish dry with paper towels. Place fillets in flour; set aside.

Coat the bottom of a large heavy skillet with $1/8$ inch of oil. Heat over medium-high heat. In shallow dish, combine egg whites, milk and seasoning. Dip both sides of floured fish in mixture; dredge in cornmeal and turn to coat well. Shake off excess. Fry 4 to 5 minutes, each side. Drain on paper towels.

Serve hot with cole slaw, baked beans, lemon slices and Texas Basic Cornbread, *recipe page 47.*

 Serves 6

Mesquite-Grilled Salmon

Salmon Croquettes

Salmon
Croquettes

If you need to stretch this recipe to serve more, add a few tablespoons of mashed potatoes or another beaten egg.

12-ounce can of salmon, drained with liquid reserved
1/2 cup finely chopped onion
1/2 cup finely chopped celery
1 cup cracker or bread crumbs
1 egg, beaten
2 to 4 tablespoons vegetable oil

Pick out any bones and skin from salmon. Mash salmon with onion, celery, crumbs and egg. Add reserved liquid 1 tablespoon at a time until mixture holds together. Form 6 patties, approximately 4 x 3/4 inches. Fry in nonstick skillet with just enough oil to prevent sticking until done.

 **Yields 6 croquettes**

Mesquite-Grilled
Salmon

Mesquite flavors this fish, the sauce is optional.

2 whole salmon, skin on, 3 to 4 pounds each
zest of 2 lemons
2 lemons, juiced
1/2 cup chopped fresh dill
1 cup white wine
1 clean cedar shingle, soaked in water

Place salmon in shallow glass dish. Mix remaining ingredients and pour over salmon. Cover with plastic wrap and let stand at least 1 hour while preparing mesquite fire.

Let mesquite coals burn down and arrange them around edges of grill. Place salmon on cedar shingle, skin side down. Place shingle in center of grill about 18 inches above coals. Cover and grill for 30 minutes.

Serve immediately with sauce on the side.

SEAFOOD SAUCE
1/2 cup Easiest and Best Mayonnaise, *recipe page 159*
1 tablespoon horseradish, grated
juice of 1 lemon

Mix well and serve with salmon.

 Serves 8

Oyster
Chowder

We get our oysters fresh from the Texas Gulf to make this warm, filling chowder. You can also substitute clams or add fish for more variety.

4 **large carrots, grated**
1 **cup chopped onions**
4 **stalks celery, chopped**
1 **medium turnip, grated**
3 **tablespoons flour**
2 **cups half-and-half**
1 **15-ounce can of cream-style corn**
4 **cups milk**
1 **cup butter, divided**
2 **pints fresh oysters**

Melt $1/2$ cup of butter in heavy skillet. Sauté carrots, onions, celery and turnip until soft. Add flour, half and half and corn. Place mixture in large stock pot and add milk. In skillet, sauté oysters in $1/2$ cup of butter; add to stock pot. Season with salt and black pepper to taste.

Serve in large soup bowls with hot bread or toast.

 Serves 12

Grilled
Marinated Shrimp

This can be an appetizer or a main course.

24 **large shrimp, peeled and deveined**

MARINADE
$1^1/2$ **cups soy sauce**
$1/4$ **cup Worcestershire sauce**
$1/3$ **cup lemon juice**
$1/4$ **cup vinegar**
$1/2$ **cup Burgundy wine**
2 **tablespoons dry mustard**
2 **teaspoons kosher salt or sea salt**
4 **tablespoons freshly ground black pepper**
2 **tablespoons chopped fresh parsley**
4 **garlic cloves, crushed**

Mix marinade ingredients in large glass or plastic container with cover. Place shrimp in marinade, cover and refrigerate for 20 to 24 hours.

Remove shrimp; discard marinade. Grill shrimp over hot coals for 2 minutes per side. Serve immediately.

 Serves 4 to 6

Jalapeño
Stuffed Shrimp

Add grilled vegetables and call these shrimp a main course. It takes practice to know when shrimp are ready, as soon as shrimp turn pink and begin to firm—take care not to overcook.

24 jumbo shrimp, peeled, deveined and butterflied
12 slices bacon, halved
3 fresh jalapeños
24 toothpicks

Cut each jalapeño lengthwise in eight strips and remove seeds. Place a strip of jalapeño in butterflied shrimp and close. Wrap ½ slice of bacon tightly around shrimp and put toothpick through bacon and shrimp to hold all together. Place on medium hot grill, turning once. Cook 2 to 3 minutes per side. Remove from grill, twist out toothpicks and eat while hot.

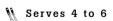 **Serves 4 to 6**

Jalapeño Stuffed Shrimp

Poblano and Red
Pepper Enchiladas

These meatless enchiladas make everyone happy—especially the vegetarians. This is a great side dish with grilled steaks.

2 to 3 large sweet onions
3 to 4 poblano peppers
2 large red sweet peppers (bells or bull's horns)
2 large yellow sweet/mild peppers (bells or large sweet banana peppers)
8 ounces Monterey Jack cheese, grated
18 tortillas
4 tablespoons corn or vegetable oil
1 recipe Green Chile Sauce, *recipe page 120*

Preheat oven to 375°.

Seed and stem peppers. Cut into narrow, 2- to 3-inch strips. Peel and slice onion into vertical strips.

In a large sauté pan, heat oil over medium-high heat. Soften the tortillas in the hot oil, just a few seconds, until pliable. Remove, blot with paper towel or brown bag, stack to keep warm. Fill each tortilla with a generous heaping tablespoon of grated cheese, a tablespoon of sliced onion, and a table-spoon of each of the three peppers. Squeeze together and roll up. Place the rolled enchiladas in a 9 x 13-inch casserole.

Pour the sauce over the top just before baking and sprinkle any extra cheese and peppers along the edges of the baking dish. Bake for 25 to 30 minutes until sauce is bubbling and peppers are tender but still have a little crispness.

Serves 8

Bell Peppers

Chiles
Rellenos

A chile relleno is a stuffed chile pepper. We recommend Anaheims, the Big Jim variety or poblanos. There are many ideas for stuffing a chile. The basic ingredient is cheese, but you may add ham, ground beef, or even seafood. The true chile relleno is fried in a heavy skillet in hot oil, but health-conscious cooks know that baking them is a heart-healthy and tasty alternative.

12 large chiles with stem, roasted and peeled (See page 138.)
1 pound cheese, cut into strips
1 pound thick-sliced ham, cut into strips

To stuff chiles, cut small slits below the stem and remove the seeds. Place strips of cheese and ham inside slit.

BATTER

4 eggs, separated	**4 tablespoons flour**
3/4 teaspoon baking powder	**1/3 teaspoon salt**

Preheat oven to 350°.

Beat egg whites until stiff, set aside. Beat yolks until thick, set aside. Sift together dry ingredients and add yolks, blending well. Carefully fold beaten egg whites into yolk mixture. Dip stuffed chile into batter, then fry in deep fat at 360° until golden brown.

Or place stuffed chiles in nonstick casserole, pour batter over them and bake in oven about 20 minutes until batter is done and slightly browned on top. Serve at once.

Serves 8

Pablano and Red Pepper Enchiladas *(top)*

Chiles Rellenos *(bottom)*

SAUCES
★

Jalapeño Marmalade Sauce

★

When the jalapeños get dark, the sauce sets up and tastes best. It can be used on any kind of meat dish.

1 15½-ounce jar orange marmalade
1½ cups pineapple juice
1 jalapeño, diced
2 tablespoons cornstarch
2 cups confectioner's sugar

In a small saucepan, empty the jar of orange marmalade, rinsing the jar with pineapple juice. Add jalapeño, cornstarch and confectioner's sugar. Stir with wire whisk until cornstarch and sugar are dissolved. Bring to boil, stirring often. Reduce heat and simmer until pepper turns dark, about 45 to 50 minutes. Serve hot over meats.

Sometimes degree of hotness needs to be adjusted with more or less jalapeño, to *your* taste. Just a good bite of pepper is what you want.

Yields 3½ cups

Jalapeño Raspberry Sauce

★

Doris Cauble's favorite sauce—raspberry, with jalapeño added to enhance it, works well with many main dishes.

3 cups fresh red raspberries
1½ cups of mango nectar
1 jalapeño, diced
2 tablespoons cornstarch
2 cups confectioner's sugar

Cook raspberries with 1 cup juice until tender, about 5 minutes. Add remaining juice, jalapeño, cornstarch and confectioner's sugar. Stir with wire whisk until cornstarch and sugar are dissolved. Bring to a boil. Reduce heat and simmer until pepper turns dark, about 45 to 50 minutes. Serve warm over poultry or pork.

Yields 4½ cups

Some Texas cooks would rather disclose their secret fishing hole than share their barbecue sauce recipe. Not us. We've borrowed from friends, learned from family members and asked for secrets. From tangy barbecue sauce to sweet glazes with a hint of jalapeño, we often add a sauce for interest to our meats or other dishes. You'll find yourself experimenting. Your outcome will improve as you add, subtract and improvise.

Jalapeño Peppers

Red Bell Pepper

Tart Honeyed Sauce

This can be used on pork, game hens, chicken breasts, chicken halves and even on dove and quail. Double this recipe for one side of pork ribs. When doubling the recipe, do not double the Tabasco because it sometimes makes it too hot.

- 1/2 cup Burgundy wine
- 1/2 cup pineapple juice
- 1/4 cup apple cider vinegar
- 1/4 cup soy sauce
- 3 tablespoons prepared mustard
- 1/2 cup honey
- 1 teaspoon Tabasco Sauce

Mix all ingredients in stainless bowl.

Yields 2 cups

Red Chile Paste

This paste is great on grilled corn or on a cracker if you really like "hot."

- 6 dried red chile peppers, anchos or New Mexico
- 1 red bell pepper, chopped
- 1 teaspoon oregano
- 1 teaspoon paprika
- 1 teaspoon cumin
- 2 cloves garlic, pressed
- 1 teaspoon salt
- 2 tablespoons apple cider vinegar
- 1 tablespoon olive oil
- 2 cups sourdough bread, torn

Boil red chile peppers in water 15 minutes. Remove stems and chop. For more heat, leave in the seeds; for less, remove seeds before chopping. Remember you can always add heat, but it's hard to cool it down. In a blender, combine chile peppers, red bell pepper, garlic, oregano, paprika, cumin and salt. Chop for 30 seconds. After all is chopped, add vinegar and olive oil. Blend while adding bread pieces.

Yields 1 cup

Red Chile Butter

Use for basting steaks, chicken or pork. It's really good tossed with fresh pasta.

- 1 pound butter, room temperature
- 3 tablespoons lemon or lime juice
- 1/2 cup West Texas Basic Red Chile Sauce, *recipe page 120*
- 1 teaspoon salt
- 1 tablespoon freshly ground black pepper

Mix butter, black pepper, salt and West Texas Basic Red Chile Sauce in blender. Pour into container and cover. Store in refrigerator for up to two weeks.

For a variation, substitute 1/2 cup chopped fresh basil for the chile sauce.

Yields 2 1/2 cups

Red Chile Butter

SAUCES

★

Green Chile Sauce

★

This sauce can be used as a smothering sauce for burritos, enchiladas or it can be spooned into tacos.

1/4 cup olive or vegetable oil
1/2 cup chopped white onion
4 tablespoons flour
1/2 teaspoon cumin
1/2 cup chicken broth
1 cup milk
1/2 teaspoon garlic salt
1/2 teaspoon black pepper
1 pound green chiles, roasted, peeled and diced (See page 138.)

In heavy saucepan, brown onion until tender. Whisk in flour and cumin. When mixture begins to brown, slowly whisk in broth and milk, stirring constantly. Add garlic salt, black pepper and green chiles. Purée all in blender. Warm and serve. Store refrigerated for 3 to 4 days.

Yields 3 cups

Green Chile Sauce

Green Chiles

West Texas Basic Red Chile Sauce

★

We use our "Basic Red" so many ways—in Chile Colorado, over enchiladas, over meatloaf, over scrambled eggs, heated with grated cheese for an awesome chile con queso— and more.

10 to 12 dried New Mexico chiles, stemmed, seeded and rinsed
4 or 5 garlic cloves
2 teaspoons cumin
2 teaspoons oregano
2 teaspoons salt
1/2 cup olive oil
4 tablespoons flour

Cover chile pods with water and boil for 10 minutes. Remove from heat and let stand for 30 minutes, reserving liquid. Transfer pods to blender and add garlic, cumin, oregano and salt. Purée, adding reserved liquid to make a smooth paste. Heat the olive oil, add flour and brown. Add chile paste. Add reserved liquid as needed to make gravy. This may be refrigerated for up to one month.

Yields approximately 2 1/2 cups

New Mexico Chiles

Barbecue Mop Sauce

This mop sauce will keep refrigerated for up to one month. Use with beef, pork or cabrito.

1/2 gallon vinegar
4 cups water
1 pound butter
4 tablespoons dry mustard
4 tablespoons salt
2 tablespoons crushed red pepper
4 tablespoons brown sugar
4 tablespoons chili powder
4 tablespoons Worcestershire sauce
4 tablespoons freshly ground black pepper
1 whole garlic pod, with root end washed well
4 cups sliced yellow onions

Bring all ingredients to boil in large stockpot for 15 minutes. Simmer for 2 hours.

For a sweeter sauce, add 1 1/2 cups of apricot preserves and 1 cup of crushed pineapple 30 minutes prior to serving.

**Yields 8 cups
(with addition of preserves and pineapple yield increases to 10 cups)**

Granddad Mickan's Barbecue Sauce

Mr. Mickan was a rancher from Copperas Cove whose family came to Texas in 1854 from Germany.

1/2 cup beef tallow
2 cups water
1 large onion
1 cup butter
1 lemon, sliced
2 cups catsup
1/2 cup Worcestershire sauce
1 tablespoon coarse-ground black pepper
1 tablespoon paprika
1 teaspoon salt

Place all ingredients in stainless saucepan and boil slowly. Remove tallow and simmer 30 minutes.

TIP: Tallow is the fatty tissue or "suet" around cuts of meat...the solid animal fat.

Yields 6 cups

Cabrito Seasoning

This may also be used on venison or lamb.

1/2 cup black pepper
1/4 cup chili powder
1/4 cup salt
2 tablespoons cumin
1 tablespoon oregano

Mix all spices. Rub the meat with olive oil to help the seasoning stick to the meat. Coat meat 2 to 3 hours before cooking.

Yields 1 cup

Onions and Garlic

SAUCES

Green Chile Salsa

This salsa is a favorite served with chips or veggies at any gathering. We really like it on our eggs, hamburgers and most meat dishes.

12 fresh green chiles, roasted, peeled and chopped
2 fresh tomatoes, diced
1 large onion, diced
1/2 teaspoon garlic salt
1/2 cup Vinaigrette Dressing, *recipe page 160*

Mix all ingredients; refrigerate covered two hours before serving.

Will keep up to one week in refrigerator.

Yields 3 to 4 cups

Mango Salsa

This is mighty good with suckling pig or cabrito.

2 cups mango, peeled and chopped
4 fresh jalapeños, seeded and chopped
2 cloves garlic, chopped
1/2 teaspoon salt
1/2 teaspoon white pepper
1/4 cup lime juice
2 tablespoons cilantro, chopped

Combine and let stand for 1 hour before serving.

Yields 2 cups

Texas Pecan Pesto

This is good made with basil or cilantro.

1 cup basil or cilantro leaves, packed
1/2 cup pecans
3 garlic pods
1 tablespoon lime juice or balsamic vinegar
1/2 cup olive oil
1/2 teaspoon salt
1 tablespoon black pepper
4 tablespoons Parmesan cheese, shredded

Add all ingredients, except cheese, to blender. Blend well. Stir in Parmesan cheese.

Serve with 1 pound of fresh pasta.

Yields approximately 1 1/4 cups

Pecans

Pico de Gallo

On the cowboy's table, this dish is more important than catsup. They eat it on their eggs in the morning, as a snack with chips, alongside any meat that we serve, atop any Mexican food dish. It's a must-have for any party, large or small.

2 cups yellow onions, chopped
4 large ripe tomatoes, chopped
6 jalapeño peppers, seeded and diced
1 teaspoon salt

Chop onions and tomatoes. Discard stems and chop jalapeño peppers. Mix all ingredients with salt. Cover and refrigerate.

Adjust the amount of peppers according to the hotness of the jalapeños.

Yields 4 cups

Prickly Pear Jelly

Texas is blessed or cursed, depending with whom you speak, with acres and acres of prickly pear cacti. In the springtime, their lemony-green pads sprout vibrant yellow and orange-red blooms. Those blooms mature to red or deep purple "pears"—mature pears are covered with thousands of tiny prickles....so harvesting is not for the faint-hearted. But any harvester willing to wield long kitchen tongs, thick rubber gloves, and a bucket will be rewarded with prickly pear fruit that can be made into a lovely jelly.

3 cups prickly pear juice
3 cups sugar
1/2 cup lemon juice
6 ounces liquid fruit pectin

Pick two gallons pear fruit using kitchen tongs and long rubber gloves. Ripe fruit will give just a little when squeezed.

Put immediately into cold water for 5 to 10 minutes. Pare, using rubber gloves. Quarter pears, place in medium saucepan and cover with water. Boil on high for 5 minutes. Pour boiled mixture through cheesecloth to strain seeds. Combine pear juice, sugar and lemon juice. Bring mixture to rolling boil, reduce heat to medium, add liquid fruit pectin and cook for 10 to 12 minutes, or until mixture begins to thicken. Skim foam from top.

You may store in sterilized canning jars sealed with paraffin or simply refrigerate to use in a sauce.

Yields 3 pints

...beans kept many from starving on the prairie.

VEGGIES, SIDES & SALADS

Always looking for authentic chuckwagon utensils, Bill Cauble began collecting antique coffee grinders. After trying many brands of coarsely ground black pepper, he never found exactly what he wanted. So he began grinding his own peppercorns—with an old coffee grinder —adjustable for coarse or fine grounds and handy when you're seasoning several hundred pounds of beef for a big party. Black pepper is a common denominator in most recipes in this section as well as in the main dish section…look for a new or an old coffee grinder to adapt for personal use.

VEGGIES & SIDE DISHES

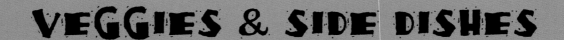

Don't worry if you don't get all of the corn silks removed.
They'll burn off quickly and won't affect the taste.

Potato Corn
Patties

Leftover baked or mashed potatoes? Combine them with fresh or leftover corn and reinvent a side dish. Or try them for breakfast with syrup.

4 to 6 cups potatoes, mashed
1 cup diced yellow onions
1 jalapeño, finely chopped
3 ears of corn, cooked
3 eggs
3 cups vegetable oil
1 teaspoon pepper
1 teaspoon salt
2 cups flour

Cut corn from cobs. Mix potatoes, corn, onion, jalapeño, eggs, salt and pepper in bowl. Place flour in dredging pan. Using a large serving spoon, dip a full spoonful of potato-corn mixture and carefully place in flour. Flatten to $1/2$-inch thickness. Turn and flour other side. In a skillet, heat $3/4$ to 1 inch of oil on medium-high heat. Fry patties in oil 2 to 3 minutes. Turn and cook 2 minutes each side. Drain on paper towels.

Serve hot.

Serves 8 to 10

Corn
Pudding

Watt Matthews's great-niece Susan Wilson fixes this to complement rib eye steaks...sure hope she likes this version.

6 ears of corn, kernels removed or 2$1/2$ cups of fresh corn
3 eggs
3 tablespoons flour
$1/2$ cup sugar
2 cups milk
$1/2$ teaspoon salt
6 tablespoons of butter

Preheat oven 350°.

Melt butter in saucepan over medium heat and stir in corn. Cook for 15 minutes, stirring often. Mix eggs, flour and sugar in bowl. Add milk, corn and salt. Pour all into nonstick 8 x 8-inch baking dish. Bake 45 minutes or until firm.

Serves 8

Jalapeño Peppers

Grilled Corn on the Cob
with Red Chile Paste

Don't worry if you don't get all of the corn silks removed. They'll burn off quickly and won't affect the taste.

6 ears fresh corn
Red Chile Paste, *recipe page 119*

Shuck corn and clean off silks. Place on hot grill. Roll often, every 3 to 4 minutes. Cook for 20 to 22 minutes. Corn will sometimes brown in spots but this just enhances the flavor.

Serve hot with Red Chile Paste.

 Serves 6

Fresh Creamed
Style Corn

With an abundance of fresh Colorado corn last year, this recipe was a hit at the Nail Western Hunt.

8 ears corn, kernels removed
1 cup butter
1 cup diced yellow onions
1 pint whipping cream
1/4 cup flour
salt and pepper to taste

Melt butter in large skillet over medium heat. Add onions and sauté until soft. Add corn, stirring often and cook for 15 to 20 minutes. Sprinkle flour over corn. Stir and cook for 5 minutes. Add whipping cream and stir until smooth. Reduce heat and simmer 5 to 10 minutes.

Serve hot.

 **Serves 8 to 10**

Fried
Corn

When removing kernels from the cob, place the skinny end of the ear into a deep bowl to catch all kernels as they are sliced off. With the dull side of the knife, scrape the cob to get all the remaining milk and pulp, taking care not to scrape off the tough husk.

**12 ears of corn, husks, silks and kernels removed
    (about 4 cups of corn)**
4 slices bacon, diced
1/2 cup onion, diced
salt and pepper to taste
1 cup half-and-half
2 tablespoons butter
1 tablespoon chili powder
lime wedges
strips of sweet red pepper for garnish

In heavy cast iron skillet, fry bacon until crisp; remove and set aside. Add onion, corn, salt and pepper to bacon drippings and fry over low heat, stirring often, for 4 to 5 minutes. Add half-and-half and butter; cover and cook over very low heat until tender. Turn out on hot platter; sprinkle with bacon bits and chili powder. Garnish with pepper strips, and lime wedges that can be squeezed over individual servings.

 Serves 6

Pinto
Beans

Pinto beans are a must at every Texas barbecue, as they were on the long trail drives to Kansas. Chuck wagon cooks knew they could stretch a pot of beans through at least a couple of meals—they were easy to serve in a tin cup if a cowboy didn't have time to sit for a meal. And they had a medicinal use: if a cowboy had a bad tooth and couldn't chew, mashed up beans kept many from starving on the prairie.

2 pounds pinto beans, picked over and washed
6 thick slices bacon, chopped
1 cup chopped yellow onions
2 cloves garlic, crushed
2 dried red chile peppers, crushed
2 tablespoons kosher salt or sea salt
water

Soak beans overnight if preferred. Brown bacon in pan used for cooking beans. Place beans, onion, garlic, chile peppers and salt in pot. Cover with water about 3 inches above beans. Bring to a vigorous boil. Reduce heat to simmer. Place lid on, but do not cover completely. It normally takes 3 to $3\frac{1}{2}$ hours until beans are soft. Check about every 30 minutes. If water is needed, add only very hot water. Taste and add more salt if needed.

TIP: If you have leftover beans, add some broth to make a hearty bean soup the next day.

Serves 18 to 20

Black
Beans

Black beans, with their unusual, deep rich color add visual and delicious interest to any plate.

1 pound black beans, picked over and washed
3 ounces salt pork, diced or several slices bacon
6 cups water
1 medium onion, coarsely chopped
2 cloves garlic, peeled and sliced
1 carrot, sliced or diced

Carefully sort beans, picking out any rocks and/or split beans. Rinse the beans well.

In a large (3 quart) Dutch oven, sauté the salt pork or bacon until crisp, reduce heat and add the onion, garlic and carrot. Cook for 2 to 3 minutes until onion becomes transparent. Add the water and beans. Bring to a boil and simmer covered for 1^1/2 to 2 hours, until the beans are tender. Stir occasionally to be sure beans are covered with liquid and do not stick...add water as needed to keep beans just covered with liquid.

Serve as a side dish or with hot steaming rice.

Serve black beans with assorted toppings of: grated cheese; chopped avocado; chopped sweet onion; diced tomato; Pico de Gallo, *recipe page 123;* shredded chicken and/or sliced steak.

 Serves 8

Green Beans
and New Potatoes

Fresh-snapped green beans used to be a treat, often saved for Sunday dinner. Today, they're available year-round. If you must, you can substitute frozen green beans, but never canned.

8 cups snapped green beans
5 cups new potatoes, skins on or 4 medium, cubed
^{1}/2 cup chopped yellow onions
8 slices thick-sliced bacon, diced
2^1/2 cups water
1 teaspoon salt
1 teaspoon cracked black pepper

Wash beans and put into 2 cups boiling water. Cover and cook until tender, about 20 to 25 minutes. As beans are cooking, brown bacon in heavy pan adding onions just before the bacon is done. After onions are soft, add potatoes and stir often with bacon and onions. After 10 to 15 minutes, add ^{1}/2 cup of water. Cover and cook until potatoes begin to soften. Add beans and bean liquid to potatoes, bacon and onions. Add salt and pepper. Cover and simmer for 20 to 25 minutes.

TIP: The dish can simmer on low heat if more time is needed for other food preparation.

 Serves 8

Butter Beans
and Ham

All beans are popular in the Southwest—and one-pot dishes are great on the wagon. This keeps warm for several hours—great if you have people eating in shifts.

2 pounds dried large Lima beans, picked over and washed
6 thick slices bacon, diced
2-pound cured, boneless ham, cubed in 2-inch pieces
1 cup diced onion
1 teaspoon salt
1 teaspoon pepper

Carefully sort beans, picking out any rocks and/or split beans. Rinse the beans well.

Place beans in medium stock pot; cover with about 2 quarts of water. Brown bacon in cast iron skillet, remove and add to beans. Brown ham in bacon drippings. Add to bean pot. Add onions, salt and pepper. Cook uncovered over medium heat for $1^1/4$ to $1^1/2$ hours, stirring occasionally. Add warm water as needed to keep beans just covered with liquid.

 Serves 12 to 14

Butter Beans and Ham

Cowboy Favorite Oven-Fried Potatoes

Cowboy Favorite
Oven-Fried Potatoes

This is easy to expand for a crowd or to reduce for a small dinner. If the potatoes are larger, they may need to be cut in thirds.

10 medium new potatoes, skin on
1/2 cup butter
1 teaspoon salt
1 teaspoon cayenne pepper
1 teaspoon chopped fresh parsley

Preheat oven to 450°.

Melt butter in oven-safe 13 x 20-inch pan or 2 smaller pans. Cut potatoes in half, lengthwise. Place cut side down in hot butter. Bake for 25 minutes, turn potatoes and cook an additional 15 minutes. Remove from oven, sprinkle with salt, cayenne pepper and parsley.

Serve hot.

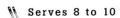 **Serves 8 to 10**

Dutch Oven
Potatoes

A good chuck wagon cook and special friend of Bill's, Howard Rogers, helped create this recipe when cooking for the crew at Abilene's Western Heritage Classic. This works really well for a large group.

6 pounds potatoes, peeled and diced in 1-inch cubes
2 cups diced yellow onions
3 pounds thick-sliced bacon, diced
3 ears corn
2 tablespoons freshly ground black pepper
1 tablespoon kosher salt or sea salt
2 1/2 cups warm water
1/4 cup chopped fresh parsley

Cut corn from cob and set aside. Brown bacon in 16-inch Dutch oven or iron skillet with cover. Just before bacon is done, add onions and cook until onions are translucent. Add potatoes, stirring often. Cook 15 to 20 minutes. Add corn, salt and pepper; stir. Add warm water. Cover and cook for 20 minutes with coals on top and bottom.

To cook in home kitchen, preheat oven to 325°.
Bake, covered, for 20 to 25 minutes.

Sprinkle fresh parsley over the top and serve.

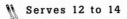 **Serves 12 to 14**

Chunky
Mashed Potatoes

Leave lumps, people will know they are real! Of course, potato flakes have their place in our kitchens. If we need to thicken a gravy or soup, we'll add a few potato flakes to do the trick.

8 large potatoes, peeled and cubed
1 cup whipping cream
1/4 cup chopped fresh parsley
1/2 cup butter, softened
1 teaspoon salt
1 teaspoon pepper

Boil potatoes in water in large stock pot until tender. Drain potatoes and place in serving bowl or pan with softened butter. Mash with potato masher, leaving lumps. Add salt, pepper and whipping cream. Stir gently. Add half of the parsley. Stir gently and add remaining parsley.

Serves 8 to 10

Scalloped
Potatoes

You'll find several potato recipes in this book simply because cowboys and crowds like them. Chuck wagon cooks used potatoes because they'd keep for months at a time.

6 potatoes, peeled and thinly sliced
2 cups half-and-half
1 1/2 cups flour
1 cup butter
1 red bell pepper, diced
1 jalapeño, diced
1 tablespoon freshly ground black pepper
milk

Preheat oven to 350°.

Rub butter on bottom of deep 3-quart baking pan or dish. Layer potatoes, red bell pepper and diced jalapeño. Sprinkle each layer with black pepper, flour and slices of butter. Continue until all vegetables, flour, butter and pepper are used. Pour half-and-half over potatoes, and fill to top layer with milk. Cover and bake for about 1 hour. Uncover and bake an additional 20 minutes.

Serves 8 to 10

Chuck wagon cooks used potatoes because they'd keep for months at a time.

Herbed New Potatoes
in Sour Cream

This recipe is from Mary Faulk Koock, who encouraged Clifford to write a cookbook in 1976. This dish was served for Lady Bird Johnson's parties at the LBJ Ranch.

3 pounds new potatoes, whole with skins
1/4 cup butter
1/4 cup sour cream
4 tablespoons finely chopped fresh parsley
1 teaspoon salt
1 tablespoon coarsely ground black pepper

Cook potatoes until just tender; drain and keep warm. In a saucepan, melt butter and sour cream. Add butter, sour cream, parsley, salt and pepper to potatoes and toss lightly until well coated.

Serve immediately.

 **Serves 8 to 10**

ROASTING GREEN CHILES

Fresh green chiles really make the difference. In preparation for your recipes and in order to preserve them in the freezer, you can roast them using the following steps. Fresh chiles can be used in salads; however, the tough outer skin makes this uncooked form undesirable in other recipes.

STEP 1:

Select chiles with large smooth pods with well-rounded smooth shoulders. The chiles should be firm, mature, thick-fleshed pods with bright shiny surfaces. Avoid shriveled, immature, dull or crooked pods.

STEP 2:

Rinse each pod with cool, fresh water. Pierce each pod with a fork to allow steam to escape during roasting.

STEP 3:

Place chile on a cookie sheet and broil 4 to 6 inches below broiler unit. Broil on high with door open; turn chiles frequently for even blistering. Chile will blacken.
OR Place chiles on hot mesquite coals until blackened. This method enhances the flavor and eliminates the mess in your kitchen.

STEP 4:

Place blackened chiles in a ziplock bag or bowl and cover with damp cup towel to steam 10 to 12 minutes.

STEP 5:

Chiles are ready to place in freezer bags for later use. To use, hold chile pod under slow-running tap water; remove skin from stem end peeling downward. Remove stem and seeds. Leave the stems intact if you are making chiles rellenos.

Pepper Facts

The Scoville hotness scale rates the heat in pepper varieties on a scale of 1 to 10. Hotness can vary within a variety or even among peppers of the same variety within the same garden plot. Use this table for comparative purposes.

Pepper Variety	Hotness Scale	Scoville Units
Habanero	10	100,000-300,000
Cayenne	8	
Tabasco	8	30,000-50,000
Serrano	6	5,000-15,000
Jalapeño	5	2,500-5,000
Ancho	3	
Pasilla	3	
New Mexico (dried)	3	1,000-1,500
Poblano	2	
Anaheim	2	
Big Jim	2	500-1,000
Mexibell	1	
Bull's horn	1	100-500
Bell	0	
Sweet Banana	0	0

Sweet Potato
Casserole

No Thanksgiving feast is complete without sweet potatoes.

**6 sweet potatoes, boiled and drained,
reserving 2/3 cup of liquid or
1 large can sweet potatoes with
2/3 cup potato juice reserved**
1/4 cup butter
1/4 cup sugar
1/4 cup milk
2 beaten eggs
2 teaspoons vanilla

Preheat oven to 350°.

Heat reserved juice. Add all ingredients and mash.
Put into 9 x 13–inch baking dish. Top with:

TOPPING
1 cup brown sugar
1/2 cup flour
1 cup chopped pecans
1/2 stick butter, melted

Mix sugar, flour and pecans; spread over potatoes.
Drizzle butter over top and bake for 30 minutes.

Serve hot.

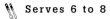 **Serves 6 to 8**

Wild Texas
Rice

Texas is a top-producer of rice. This rice dish is popular with our Beef Tips and Beef Stroganoff. If there's any left over, add chicken stock, some vegetables and a little meat and you have a hearty soup.

2 cups long grain rice
1 cup wild rice
6 cups chicken stock
1 teaspoon salt
2 tablespoons butter

Combine all ingredients in large saucepan with tight-fitting lid. Bring to boil and stir. Reduce heat. Cover tightly and simmer 45 to 50 minutes. Remove from heat and let rest 10 minutes.

Serve piping hot.

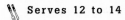 **Serves 12 to 14**

Macaroni
with Bacon

Bill's Aunt Ann Newcomb served this as a main dish—with bread. Of course, there was no original recipe, so it took a few testings on the cowboys at Lambshead to perfect it. If you have leftovers, add some pinto beans the next day—for a different dish.

3 cups large elbow macaroni, cooked
10 slices thick-sliced bacon, diced
2 cups diced yellow onion
15-ounce can whole tomatoes
10-ounce can diced tomatoes with green chiles
2 15-ounce cans tomato sauce
salt and pepper to taste

Cook macaroni according to package directions. While macaroni is cooking, sauté bacon in large skillet over medium heat. Just before bacon is completely browned, add onions and cook until soft. Drain cooked macaroni and stir into bacon and onions. Reduce heat. Add whole and green chile tomatoes. Stir and cook for 5 minutes. Add tomato sauce and simmer for 15 to 20 minutes.

Serve hot.

Serves 8 to 10

Homemade
Egg Noodles

These are a staple on German and Czech menus across Texas. To serve, toss with butter and freshly ground black pepper.

12 eggs
1 tablespoon salt
12 cups flour

Beat eggs and salt in a large bowl until salt is dissolved. Gradually mix in flour. Mix until dough is stiff. If dough is sticky to touch, continue to add flour until no stickiness remains. Divide dough into four or five balls. Roll each ball on floured surface to $1/8$-inch thickness. When all balls are rolled out, dust first ball with flour. Beginning at one edge, roll into tube shape. Cut tube into $1/4$-inch slices. Unroll each strip and set aside. Repeat until all balls are cut. You may freeze or cook immediately by boiling in water or chicken broth.

Serves 8 to 10

Green Chile

Fresh Green Chile
Hominy

This was developed for the Texas Trails
Chuck Wagon back in the '70s.

4 15-ounce cans white hominy, drained, reserving
   half of the juice
10 thick slices bacon, diced
2 cups diced onions
1 cup sour cream
$1/2$ pound sharp Cheddar cheese, grated
8 fresh green chiles, roasted, peeled and diced

Preheat oven to 325°.

Crisply fry bacon in medium skillet; remove. Sauté onions in
bacon drippings until soft. Heat hominy in saucepan. Add
reserved juice to hominy; add sour cream and half of the
cheese. When cheese melts, add onions, half of the peppers,
and half of the bacon. Mix. Pour into 9 x 13-inch baking dish.
Sprinkle with remaining bacon, peppers and cheese.
Bake 15 minutes until cheese melts.

Serves 10 to 12

Fresh Green Chile Hominy

Squash Casserole

Summer Squash
Casserole–*Calabacitos*

Calabacitos translates to "tender little squash." When draining squash, it may take two or more times to remove all water. The drier the squash is, the better the dish. If there's any left over, you can add cooked, chopped chicken and broth to make soup.

3 **pounds yellow squash, cut in thin rounds**
1¹/2 **pounds zucchini squash, cut in thin rounds**
2 **cups chopped yellow onions**
1 **large red bell pepper, seeded and chopped**
¹/2 **cup water**
1 **pound sharp Cheddar cheese, grated**
5 **ears corn, kernels cut and scraped from cob**
3 **fresh jalapeño peppers, seeded and finely chopped**
¹/2 **teaspoon salt**
2 **cups sour cream**

Preheat oven to 350°.

In a large Dutch oven, cook the squash, onions and bell pepper in ¹/2 cup of water over medium heat, until tender. Drain liquid and mash with a potato masher. Add the cheese, corn, jalapeños, salt and sour cream. Stir to mix well. Pour into a buttered 12-inch cake pan or 9 x 13-inch baking dish. Sprinkle cheese on top. Bake until bubbly or starting to brown.

Serve immediately.

Serves 12 to 14

Grilled
Eggplant

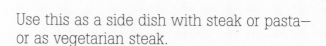

Use this as a side dish with steak or pasta— or as vegetarian steak.

1 **eggplant, sliced 1-inch thick**
1¹/2 **cup olive oil**
1 **tablespoon balsamic vinegar**
2 **tablespoons coarsely ground black pepper**
1 **tablespoon salt**
1 **teaspoon cayenne pepper**
2 **garlic cloves, minced**

Combine oil, vinegar and seasoning; mix well. Brush eggplant with mixture; let stand 30 minutes. Grill over mesquite coals, 12 to 15 inches above coals, for 10 minutes. Turn, grill 10 minutes until tender.

Serves 2

Grilled
Mixed Vegetables

This festive dish offers lots of color and pairs well with beef tenderloin—and it's the only vegetable you'll need to serve.

3 red bell peppers
3 orange or yellow bell peppers
2 green bell peppers
1½ cups mushrooms, halved
2 cups yellow onions
4 zucchini squash, cut in ¼-inch cubes
1½ cups Vinaigrette Dressing, *recipe page 160*
1 tablespoon fresh ground black pepper
1 teaspoon kosher salt or sea salt
2 large grilling baskets

Halve bell peppers, remove core and veins and cut in long thin slices. Peel outer skin on onions, place root side down and cut in half from top to bottom, slice halves for long slivers. Place all vegetables in 1 or 2 grilling baskets, assuring a medium thickness of vegetables. Pour all dressing over vegetables and let stand about 20 minutes. Cook over hot coals, stirring often. Peppers and onions should become quite limp after about 15 to 20 minutes.

Remove from grill. Salt and pepper and serve immediately.

Serves 12 to 14

Sautéed
Spinach

Fresh spinach is great in salads, but this is a quick and easy way to serve it warm.

¼ cup olive oil
2 garlic cloves, minced
1 pound fresh spinach, washed
1 teaspoon salt

In a 10-inch skillet or saucepan, slightly brown garlic in olive oil. Add spinach and salt; sauté until tender.

Serve immediately.

Serves 2

Bell Peppers

Turnip Greens
and Turnips

Substitute mustard or collard greens or use a mixture of all three. You may also add three or four diced turnips to the greens as they cook. No matter, Best Basic Cornbread is a must.

3/4 pound lean salt pork or thick-sliced bacon, diced
**4 1/2 pounds fresh turnip greens, trimmed, rinsed well
  and coarsley chopped**
1 1/2 cups water
1 cup chopped yellow onions
1 teaspoon sugar
salt and fresh ground black pepper to taste

In a Dutch oven, fry salt pork or bacon just until cooked. Drain, reserving 2 tablespoons of drippings. Stir in remaining ingredients and bring to a boil. Reduce heat, cover and simmer for 45 minutes or until greens are tender.

Turnips

8 turnips, tennis ball-sized, peeled and chopped
4 tablespoons butter
salt and freshly ground pepper to taste

In a medium saucepan, place turnips with water to cover. Bring to a boil and cook until just tender when pierced with a paring knife. Drain, reserving cooking liquid. Return turnips to saucepan with butter and sauté quickly for 3 minutes. Season with salt and pepper. Serve with turnip greens or as a separate vegetable to accompany roast meats.

 Serves 8 to 10

Turnip Greens and Turnips

Fried
Okra

This isn't a hard-fried okra that most are accustomed to. It's very tasty and can be cooked in large quantities and frozen in plastic bags for later use.

2 pounds okra, cut into $1/2$-inch rounds
1 cup milk or buttermilk
1 cup cornmeal
$1/2$ cup flour
salt and pepper
$1^{1}/2$ cups vegetable oil

Put cut okra into milk to ensure the corn meal mixture adheres to okra. Mix corn meal, flour, salt and pepper. Coat okra with meal mixture. Shake off excess and place in skillet with medium-hot oil. After okra begins to cook, cover skillet and cook slowly, stirring occasionally. You may have to add more oil. Cook until tender and slightly brown. Drain on paper towels before serving hot.

 Serves 6

Okra
Gumbo

If you want a one-dish meal, add sliced smoked sausage when you add the cabbage.

6 thick slices bacon, diced
$1^{1}/2$ cups diced onion
1 head cabbage, shredded
1 tablespoon salt
2 cups sliced okra
2 large tomatoes, chopped
2 tablespoons black pepper
1 pound smoked sausage, optional

Fry bacon in skillet; add onion and cook until tender. Add cabbage and salt. Simmer until cabbage wilts. Add okra and tomatoes. Cook until okra is just tender. Add pepper and salt to taste.

 **Serves 4 to 6**

Black-Eyed Peas
and Okra

We often have *both* fresh from the garden.
Watt's comment was, "If you don't like it,
don't eat it."

- **4 cups fresh or frozen black-eyed peas**
- **2 cups fresh or frozen cut okra**
- **4 slices bacon, cut into 1-inch pieces**
- **1 cup chopped yellow onions**
- **1 teaspoon black pepper**
- **1 teaspoon salt**

Fry bacon in saucepan; add onion and sauté. Add peas,
black pepper and salt. Cover with water and bring to a
boil. Simmer for 30 minutes until peas are tender, add
okra; simmer for 15 minutes. Serve immediately.

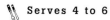 Serves 4 to 6

Black-Eyed Peas and Okra

SALADS & SOUPS

When adding dressing, stop before you think it's enough...
too much weighs down the greens.

Cornbread
Salad

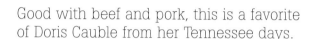

Good with beef and pork, this is a favorite of Doris Cauble from her Tennessee days.

8-inch skillet of prepared cornbread,
   may be cooked a day ahead of time
12 slices bacon, cooked crisply and crumbled
3 cups tomatoes, chopped
1 cup bell pepper, chopped (green, red, yellow
   or combination)
1 cup finely chopped onions
1/2 cup sweet pickles, chopped
1/4 cup of sweet pickle juice
1 cup Easiest and Best Mayonnaise, *recipe page 159*

Crumble half of cornbread into large serving bowl. In another bowl, combine tomatoes, bell pepper, onions, pickles and bacon; mix well. Spoon half of mixture over crumbled cornbread. In another bowl, combine mayonnaise and pickle liquid; mix well. Spread half of this mixture over the vegetables. Repeat layering with the remaining cornbread, vegetables and dressing. Cover tightly and refrigerate at least 2 hours before serving.

Serve as salad, vegetable *and* bread on hot summer evenings with grilled steaks or chicken.

 Serves 8

Spinach Salad
with Hot Dressing

A Southern tradition…the hot dressing with bacon marries well with the crisp spinach leaves.

8 ounces fresh spinach, washed, dried,
   with thick stems and veins removed
6 slices bacon, cooked and crumbled with
   1/4 cup drippings reserved for dressing
1/4 cup golden raisins
4 ounces fresh mushrooms, thinly sliced
1 cup croutons

Tear spinach into bite-sized pieces and place in salad bowl. Add bacon, raisins, mushrooms and croutons. Toss and set aside. Prepare dressing.

Serve with any steak.

HOT DRESSING
1/4 cup bacon drippings
1/4 cup red wine vinegar
1/4 cup Easiest and Best Mayonnaise, *recipe page 159*
1/4 cup sugar

Add all ingredients in a saucepan and stir to combine. Cook over low heat until very hot. While hot, pour over salad and toss to coat evenly.

Serve immediately.

Serves 4

Broccoli
Salad

Good friends and Matthews family members Jean and Glen Reynolds served this many times at the river camp.

6 stalks broccoli, tops and stems
8 to 10 slices bacon, crisply cooked and crumbled
1/2 cup raisins
4 green onions, thinly sliced
1 cup walnuts or pecans, broken into pieces

Remove tops from broccoli stems; separate. To use the broccoli stems, parboil for about 3 minutes to tenderize; peel tough fibers away and slice thinly. Mix all and add dressing 30 minutes before serving.

BROCCOLI DRESSING
1 cup Easiest and Best Mayonnaise
2 tablespoon apple cider vinegar
1/2 cup sugar

Mix dressing well.

 Serves 8

Green
Salad

When adding dressing, stop before you think it's enough...too much weighs down the greens. For variations to this salad, add grape-sized tomatoes, 1/4 cup of cashews and 1/4 cup of dried cranberries.

1 head romaine lettuce
1 head green leaf lettuce
1 pound baby leaf spinach
1 red onion, thinly sliced
1 tablespoon coarsely ground black pepper
Vinaigrette Dressing, *recipe page 160*

Wash lettuces and spinach; dry in salad spinner. Tear in bite-sized pieces, leaving some stem. In large salad bowl, toss spinach and lettuce. Add half of the onion, half of the pepper and Vinaigrette Dressing. Arrange the remaining sliced onions on top and sprinkle with remaining pepper.

 Serves 12

When adding dressing,
stop before you think it's enough.

Onion Cucumber
Salad

This works well on a hot Texas summer evening—and it's easy to put together.

2 large Texas 1015's onions
3 cucumbers, halved and seeded, unpeeled
2 quarts ice cubes
1 pint vinegar
$1/2$ cup salt
$1/2$ cup sugar

Slice Texas 1015 onions and cucumbers. Layer with ice, pour on vinegar. Add salt and sugar.

The vegetables crisp up in the ice/water bath and are wonderful for a light supper or cool lunch.

 Serves 8

Onion Cucumber Salad

Green Salad with Fruit

Green Salad
with Fruit

Sweet, tart fruit is *the* refreshing addition to any green salad. Nice for summer evenings or anytime.

1 head green leaf lettuce, torn in pieces
1/2 cup sliced red onion
1 cup fruit, sliced (pears, apples, mandarin oranges or grapefruit)
1/4 cup almonds, toasted and slivered

Slice fruit and toss with remaining ingredients. Divide into individual serving bowls.

Dress with Lynne's Salad Dressing, *recipe page 160.*

Serves 6

Fresh
Fruit Salad

When we make fruit salad, we make a bunch. If you serve it with dinner, you don't have to have a dessert. Then after sitting overnight with flavors melding, it's great for breakfast.

4 cups red seedless grapes, halved lengthwise
4 cups green seedless grapes, halved lengthwise
6 cups fresh strawberries, quartered
1 fresh pineapple, peeled, cored and diced
2 cups sliced oranges
1/2 cup sugar

In a large salad bowl, mix strawberries, grapes, pineapple and oranges. Add sugar and stir. Refrigerate at least 2 hours before serving. The longer, the better.

Serve cold.

Serves 12 to 14

Then after sitting overnight with flavors melding, it's great for breakfast.

Cowboy
Potato Salad

Even hard-to-please cowboys like this version.

4 cups potatoes, peeled and cut in 1-inch cubes
1 cup Easiest and Best Mayonnaise, *recipe page 159*
1/4 cup prepared mustard
6 hard-boiled eggs, peeled and diced
4 green onions, chopped
1 cup sweet pickles, diced
1/4 cup sweet pickle juice
2 tablespoons celery seed
salt and pepper, to taste

Cover potatoes with water in medium-sized pan and cook until just tender. Drain and rinse with cold water. Add eggs, green onions, sweet pickles, pickle juice and celery seed. Toss gently; add mayonnaise and mustard. Toss gently again until thoroughly mixed. Salt and pepper to taste.

Refrigerate and serve chilled.

 Serves 8 to 10

German
Potato Salad

Both sides of Clifford Teinert's family came to America through Galveston in 1854. This recipe came with them.

6 medium potatoes, boiled in jackets
1 cup chopped onion
6 slices bacon, diced
1/2 cup white vinegar
2 teaspoons salt
1 tablespoon black pepper
2 tablespoons sugar (optional)
1/2 cup warm water

In large bowl, peel and slice boiled potatoes while warm. Fry bacon until crisp; add onions and cook until tender. Pour mixture over potatoes. Add vinegar, salt, pepper and water. Mix well.

Serve warm.

Serves 6

Warm
Potato Salad

This is another easy dish, as well as attractive.
We suggest new potatoes fresh from the garden.

2 pounds red potatoes, cut into chunks
1 cup Easiest and Best Mayonaise, *recipe page 159*
1/4 cup Dijon mustard
3/4 cup chopped red onion
2 green onions, sliced, including tops
2 cloves garlic, minced
1 tablespoon dill weed
1/4 teaspoon lemon juice
salt and pepper to taste
fresh parsley for garnish

In a saucepan, cover potatoes with water and cook until
tender. Drain and cool slightly. Combine remaining
ingredients and add to potatoes, tossing to coat.

Serve warm.

Serves 8

Warm Potato Salad

Guacamole

Guacamole

Some like smooth guacamole, but once you eat our chunky-style, it's hard to go back.

4 medium ripe avocados
1/2 cup diced yellow onion
2 medium tomatoes, diced
4 tablespoons fresh lime juice
1 teaspoon salt
1 fresh serrano pepper, diced

Cut avocados in half lengthwise. Remove seed with knife. Using a sharp spoon, remove inside of avocados. In a small salad bowl, mash avocados with fork but leave chunky. Add all other ingredients and mix with fork. Chill and serve.

Serve with chips or on a plate as a salad.

Serves 6 to 8

Serrano Pepper

Refrigerator
Slaw

Use a grater or an electric shredder to quickly prep this salad.

1 large head cabbage, shredded
1 cup shredded onion
1 bell pepper, chopped
6 green olives, pitted and sliced
1/2 cup sugar
1/2 cup vegetable oil
1 cup white vinegar
1 teaspoon celery seed
1 teaspoon salt
1 teaspoon dried mustard

Combine cabbage, onion, pepper and olives. Sprinkle with sugar but do not stir. Combine other ingredients and bring to boil in saucepan. Boil for 3 minutes. Let cool and pour over slaw. Stir well and refrigerate, covered, for at least 24 hours.

Serves 6 to 8

Salpicon

Yet another great hot summer evening meal. Works well with most cuts of leftover beef, especially tenderloin.

3 cups cooked beef (leftover pot roast, tenderloin), sliced in 1/4-inch slices
1 cup sliced Texas 1015 onions
1/2 cup sliced jalapeños
1 cup diced ripe tomatoes
1/2 cup diced red pepper, mild or bell
2 avocados, diced
1 1/2 cups Vinaigrette Dressing, *recipe page 160*

Arrange ingredients attractively in a serving dish. Drizzle dressing evenly over all. If time permits, chill before serving.

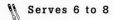 **Serves 6 to 8**

Tomato with Mozzarella and Fresh Basil

Vine-ripened tomatoes fresh from the garden taste better with fresh mozzarella and basil. This makes a tasty appetizer or side dish for a summer evening meal.

tomatoes, sliced 1/4 to 1/2 inch thick
mozzarella cheese, 1/4 inch thick
basil leaves
freshly ground black pepper, to taste

Season tomatoes with black pepper. Top with slice of mozzarella and a basil leaf.

Serve two slices of tomato and cheese per person

eño Pepper

Red Bell Pepper

DRESSINGS

We've assembled a sampling of the basic salad dressing recipes we think any cook should know how to prepare. But that assembly wasn't entirely easy. For example, finalizing Mrs. Brittingham's Dressing created a search that Sherlock Holmes would've admired. The many phone calls were worth it. We've found it's worth the extra steps—and cost-effective, too—to make our dressings from scratch.

Basil

Easiest and Best Mayonnaise

If you see how easy and refreshingly good homemade mayonnaise can be, you won't want "store-bought" mayo any more.

1 fresh egg
3 tablespoons fresh lemon juice *or* fresh lime juice or vinegar
$1/2$ teaspoon salt
1 cup vegetable oil
(we like a half and half combination of corn oil and olive oil)

Optional:
$1/2$ cup fresh parsley or basil leaves

Place egg, mustard, lemon juice and salt in food processor or blender. Pulse until well blended and a little foamy. Continue to blend, pouring oil in slowly. Add herb leaves if desired and pulse to chop and blend...just a little...so that you see the flecks of green.

Use for cold salads and as salad dressing for fresh tomatoes and other vegetables.

Refrigerate immediately to chill. Serve cold. Keeps for up to 3 days in refrigerator.

Yields $1^{1/4}$ cup

Lucille Brittingham's French Dressing

Mrs. Brittingham always served this at Lambshead Ranch. It took several phone calls quizzing family members and friends about their memories of the ingredients before we got it right. It was worth the tracking down.

$3/4$ cup olive oil
$1/2$ cup lemon juice
1 teaspoon salt
1 teaspoon paprika
1 teaspoon Dijon mustard

Shake together in covered container. It will keep refrigerated for 3 to 5 days.

Serve with any tossed green salad.

Yields $1^{1/4}$ cups

DRESSINGS

Lynne's Salad Dressing

Use lemon juice instead of vinegar when preparing this dressing for a salad with fruit.

1 cup olive oil
1 cup balsamic vinegar *or*
  1 cup lemon juice
1/2 teaspoon salt
2 garlic cloves, crushed with garlic press
1 teaspoon coarsely ground black pepper
1/4 cup grated Parmesan or crumbled
  feta cheese

Shake in container and store in refrigerator. Keeps well.

Serves 20

Limette or Lemonette Dressing

3/4 cup oil
3/4 cup lemon juice or fresh lime juice
1 tablespoon Dijon mustard
1 teaspoon salt
1 teaspoon pepper
1 teaspoon sugar

Combine all ingredients. Shake well before using.

Yields 1 1/2 cups

Lambshead Ranch Dressing

There's a reason Ranch Dressing is aptly named...a cowboy will choose it over any offered. Once you've made it from scratch, bottled versions pale in comparison.

1/3 cup vinegar
2/3 cup buttermilk
1/2 teaspoon salt
1/2 teaspoon freshly ground black pepper
1/2 teaspoon dried oregano
1/2 teaspoon chopped fresh parsley
1 clove garlic, pressed or finely minced

Optional:
1 teaspoon chopped fresh basil
1 teaspoon chopped fresh cilantro

Shake well and chill before serving.

Yields 1 cup

Cilantro

Vinaigrette Dressing

2 to 3 cloves garlic, pressed
1 teaspoon honey
kosher salt or sea salt to taste
1 tablespoon balsamic vinegar
1/4 cup olive oil

Blend all ingredients and allow time to for flavors to incorporate. Shake well before using. Will keep one week in tightly sealed, refrigerated container. Let blend overnight to marry flavors.

Yields 3/8 cup

Honey Mustard Dressing for a Crowd

1 cup honey
1 cup prepared mustard
4 1/2 cups mayonnaise
1 1/2 teaspoon paprika
1 1/2 teaspoon crushed red pepper

Combine all ingredients and blend thoroughly.

Serves 50

Cold
Tomato Soup

This easy-to-prepare dish is coolly refreshing after a long hot day outside.

3 cups chopped fresh tomatoes
$1/2$ cup chopped green or Texas 1015 onions
1 cup unpeeled shredded cucumber
$1/2$ cup fresh basil leaves
$1/2$ cup water
$1/4$ cup vinegar
$1/4$ cup olive oil
salt and pepper to taste
1 garlic clove, finely minced and blended until smooth

Mix all in medium-sized bowl and serve at room temperature or chilled.

Serve with toasted biscuits.

Serves 4 to 6

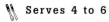

Cold Tomato Soup

Butternut Squash Soup

Butternut
Squash Soup

Serve hot topped with a spoonful of whipping cream; or Pico de Gallo, *recipe page 123*; or chopped pecans; or chopped cilantro; or sprinkled with a little fresh chile powder. Some folks like this soup served cold topped with a spoonful of yogurt or chopped cucumber.

2 pounds winter squash, butternut, acorn, pumpkin etc.
1 large onion
2¹/₂ cups chicken broth
1 cup milk
salt and pepper to taste

Preheat oven to 375°.

Halve squash, scoop out seeds, and place cut side down in a large baking dish. Cut onion in half and place cut side down in the baking dish.

Bake squash and onion until squash is tender and soft to the touch, about 30 to 45 minutes.

Scoop out the squash from its skin; peel away the onion skin. Process the roasted vegetables in batches, placing 2 cups of squash and onion in a food processor or blender with 1 cup of broth and pulse until smooth. Pour into a large saucepan. Process the remaining squash and onion in food processor with 1 cup of broth and add to the saucepan. Add other ingredients and adjust seasonings to taste.

Heat the soup, stirring frequently, but do not boil. Serve immediately in warmed soup bowls.

Serves 8 to 12

Potato
Soup

This is another recipe that started out as a way to use leftover potatoes. It's a chilly night family favorite now. Just have crackers or toasted bread to accompany.

4 medium potatoes, peeled and diced into 1-inch cubes
6 ribs celery, diced
1 celery heart, diced
2 cups diced yellow onions
1 teaspoon salt
4 tablespoons butter
2 cups milk
8 sprigs fresh parsley, chopped

Place potatoes, celery, onions and salt in stockpot with enough water to cover. Cook over medium heat until potatoes are tender; drain. Add butter and milk. Warm on low heat until milk comes to a boil. Stir with spoon until desired thickness is reached.

Serve hot. Sprinkle chopped parsley on top of each bowl when serving.

Serves 6 to 8

Add whipped cream, butter and
whiskey to regular peach cobbler.

DESSERTS

Acowboy must have meat and bread, but he'll never turn down a sweet at meal's end. Chuck wagon cooks often had to guard the sugar bowl from assault from a sugar-craving cowpoke. We don't scrimp on sugar and flour for the recipes in this section. Like the chuck wagon cooks of old, we adapt when necessary, using fresh peaches or even tomatoes in desserts. Bread pudding, which began as a way to use day-old bread, is an oft-requested dish that we never tire of preparing.

Pear-Apple Crunch

Pear-Apple
Crunch

One year there was a bounty of pears, which prompted this recipe's development. Mixing apples and pears together is always a hit.

10 to 11 fresh-picked large very firm pears, peeled and quartered or a mixture of pears and unpeeled sliced tart apples
3 tablespoons Triple sec
3/4 cup pecans, chopped

C R U N C H
2 cups sugar
2 cups flour
1 cup butter
1/2 teaspoon salt

Preheat oven 350°.

Core and slice each quartered pear crossways into 4 to 5 pieces. Place all slices in 12-inch round cake pan or 9 x 13-inch baking dish. Pour Triple sec over pears and stir so all pieces are coated. Let rest 30 minutes. Add walnuts and stir again.

Mix crunch of sugar, flour and butter in a round-bottomed bowl. Cut in butter with pastry cutter. Sprinkle mixture on top of pears. Bake 55 to 60 minutes.

Serve warm with feta, brie or sharp Cheddar crumbled on top.

TIP: Firm, slightly underripe pears are best for cooking flavor and texture. Use the very ripe pears for salads and eating out of hand.

Serves 8 to 10

Baked
Apples

A twist for fresh fruits, different fillings also work.

6 Granny Smith apples, peeled
6 teaspoons brown sugar
2 cinnamon sticks
1/4 cup Red Chile Butter, *recipe page 119*

Preheat oven to 350°.

Core apples from top, leaving bottom solid. Place 1 teaspoon brown sugar in each apple topped with 2 teaspoons of Red Chile Butter. Break cinnamon stick in 1 1/4-inch pieces and place one piece in center of apple. Bake on nonstick pan for 20 minutes. Remove cinnamon stick before serving.

 Serves 6

Apple Raisin
Crisp

Raisins are regularly used because of their long shelf life. They certainly complement apples.

12 Granny Smith apples, peeled and sliced
6 ounces golden raisins
1 cup sugar
1 teaspoon cinnamon
dash of nutmeg

Place sliced apples and raisins in 14-inch bread pan. Add cinnamon, nutmeg and sugar. Stir.

TOPPING
1 cup sugar
1 cup brown sugar
2 cups all-purpose flour
1 cup butter

Cut flour and sugars into butter with pastry cutter until mixture resembles coarse cornmeal. Sprinkle over top of apples.

Bake in 16-inch Dutch oven or large Pyrex baking dish for 40 to 45 minutes.

 Serves 16

Chuck wagon cooks typically used dried or canned fruits or whatever they found along the trail.

Peach or Apple Pie
with Pie Crust

Everyone's favorite. The last ones in line will get only fruit because the crust goes first. A scoop of ice cream on top of warm cobbler is a good combination.

**5 or 6 large firm peaches or
tart apples, peeled and thinly sliced**
3/4 cup sugar
2 tablespoons flour, rounded
3/4 teaspoon cinnamon
1/4 cup butter, cut into 12 pats
dough for two pie crusts

Preheat oven to 375°.

Place peaches or apples in unbaked pie shell. Mix sugar, flour and cinnamon; sprinkle over fruit. Dot with butter. Cover with remaining pie crust. Crimp upper and lower pie crusts to seal; slit top crust 8 to 10 times. For variation, cut into strips and lace strips for upper crust; sprinkle with cinnamon. Bake at 375° for 15 minutes; lower temperature to 350°, bake for 45 minutes or until pie bubbles and crust is browned.

Serve warm.

PIE CRUST
2 cups all-purpose flour
1 teaspoon salt
3/4 cup butter or shortening
6 tablespoons cold water

Mix salt and flour. Add butter, blend with pastry knife. Begin adding cold water to make a soft dough. Roll out on floured board.

 Serves 8

Peach Pie Crust

Fruited Sourdough Rolls

Fruited
Sourdough Rolls

Sourdough lends itself well to sweet breads. Chuck wagon cooks typically used dried or canned fruits or whatever they found along the trail. We use whatever's in season or what we find in the pantry.

1 recipe Sourdough Biscuits, *recipe page 40*
1 cup butter
1 cup sugar
2 cups dried apricots, boiled in a little water until soft
1 cup confectioner's sugar
vegetable oil

Preheat oven to 400°.

Roll Sourdough out on well-floured surface until it is about 18 to 20 inches long and 8 to 10 inches wide. Quarter butter lengthwise. Place quarter cuts of butter end to end the length of dough, about 1 inch from edge nearest to you. Repeat placing the butter quarters just past the middle of the dough. Spread apricots on each side of both rows of butter. Sprinkle sugar over entire roll. Roll entire roll away from you using first row of quartered butter as guide. (This gets easier after doing several times.) Cut with sharp knife into 1¹/₂-inch rolls. Carefully oil both sides or cut rolls and place in nonstick, large, deep baking pan or 16-inch Dutch oven. Pat down as you would sourdough rolls. Cook 20 to 25 minutes.

Mix confectioner's sugar with 1 tablespoon water until smooth. Pour over rolls when removed from oven. Let rest 5 minutes before serving.

Makes 12 to 14 rolls

TIP: Apricot preserves may be used in place of dried apricots. Or use two thinly sliced Granny Smith apples with 1 cup of golden raisins and 1 teaspoon of cinnamon. The rolls cut more easily if the apples lie parallel with the butter.

Bourbon
Peach Cobbler

This was developed for a chuck wagon competition at Fort Concho in San Angelo, Texas. It took first place. As others learned about adding whipped cream, butter and whiskey to regular peach cobbler, the recipe has become a mainstay at chuck wagon cookoffs.

1 **Cobbler Crust,** *recipe page 173*
1 **cup sugar**
6 **cups fresh peaches, peeled and sliced**
1 **cup butter**
1 **cup brown sugar**
1 **teaspoon cinnamon**
$^1/_2$ **cup Jack Daniel's Black Label Tennessee Whiskey**
$1^1/_2$ **cups whipping cream**

Preheat oven to 350°.

Melt butter in saucepan. Add peaches, brown sugar, cinnamon, sugar and cream. Bring to a boil and simmer for 10 minutes. Add whiskey and stir tenderly. Cook for 15 to 20 minutes.

Line the 9 x13-inch Pyrex dish with Cobbler Crust. Pour in fruit mixture. Cover top with either whole crust or strips of crust in latticework pattern. Bake for 45 to 50 minutes.

 Serves 8

COBBLER CRUST
2 cups flour
$^1/_2$ teaspoon salt
1 teaspoon baking powder
1 teaspoon sugar
6 tablespoons shortening
$^1/_4$ cup cold water

Mix dry ingredients, add shortening and cut in with two knives or pastry blender. Mixture should resemble coarse corn meal. Add cold water gradually to make a ball. Divide into two balls for top and bottom 9 x 13-inch cobbler crust. Roll out on floured surface with rolling pin. Place one crust in bottom of pan, add filling. Top with remaining crust or strips of crust in latticework pattern.

Lemon-Lime Sauce

Bread Pudding with Lemon-Lime Sauce

Bread Pudding
with **Lemon-Lime Sauce**

This decadent favorite is a great way to use up day-old stale bread—which is probably why it originated. It has many variations, according to your whims and what's on hand. If you don't have nuts and raisins, use fresh berries or dark chocolate.

6 cups white bread, cubed
4 cups milk
6 eggs
1½ cups sugar
2 tablespoons vanilla
½ cup unsalted butter
1 cup golden raisins
½ cup walnuts or pecans, chopped
1 tablespoon cinnamon
2 tablespoons sugar

Preheat oven to 350°.

Place cubed white bread in 9 x 13-inch baking dish or pan. Sprinkle the golden raisins and chopped nuts on top. Mix remaining ingredients in saucepan and heat on low heat until butter melts. Pour mixture over the bread, mashing the bread into the fluid. Let stand 15 minutes or until fluid is absorbed. Bake 30 minutes. Thoroughly mix together 1 tablespoon cinnamon and 2 tablespoons sugar and sprinkle on top of pudding. Bake an additional 15 minutes or until firm to the touch.

Spoon warm Lemon-Lime Sauce on top and serve warm or cold.

Serves 10 to 12

Lemon-Lime Sauce

The tartness of the lemons and the sugary sweetness make this a solid standard. The zest heightens the flavor and fragrance.

4 cups sugar   **6 eggs**
1 cup butter   **6 lemons or limes**

In saucepan, pour juice of 6 lemons and zest of 4 lemons over sugar. Over low heat, add butter and eggs, slightly beating and stirring until it thickens. When sugar is dissolved, remove from heat and serve over ice cream or bread pudding. Sprinkle the zest of remaining lemons or limes over the top.

White Chocolate Sauce

White chocolate is distinctly different from dark chocolate because it contains no cocoa solids. For best quality, choose a creamy white chocolate as opposed to a stark white chocolate.

3 ounces white chocolate
1/4 cup butter
2 tablespoons milk

Melt butter and milk in saucepan. Add white chocolate. Stir often. When chocolate melts, serve hot over pudding.

Yields 1 cup

White Chocolate Almond
Bread Pudding

Use an electric food chopper to chop almonds, and add white chocolate slowly so that it does not clump.

6 cups white bread, crusts removed
4 cups milk
6 eggs
1 1/2 cups sugar
2 tablespoons vanilla
1/2 cup butter
2 cups almonds, chopped
3 ounces white chocolate

Preheat oven to 350°.

Use thin-sliced white bread cut into 3/4 to 1-inch cubes. Place cubes in 12-inch round cake pan or 11 x 14-inch baking dish. Chop almonds and 3 ounces of white chocolate in food processor. Sprinkle almond and white chocolate mixture on bread.

Beat eggs with electric mixer in medium pan (2-quart pan or larger). Add sugar, vanilla, milk and butter. Heat on low. Butter will float, so stir often. When butter melts, remove from heat and pour over bread. Mash bread down with large spoon to absorb fluid. Let stand 15 minutes. Stir mixture lightly to distribute almonds and white chocolate. Bake for 45 to 50 minutes or until firm. Remove from oven and let rest 5 to 10 minutes.

Serve hot or cold with White Chocolate Sauce.

 Serves 10 to 12

Mary's
Sand Tarts

Called Mexican Wedding Cookies by some, these are very light and tasty, whether hot from the oven or straight from the freezer.

1 **cup butter**
1/2 **cup sifted confectioner's sugar**
2 **cups cake flour, sifted**
1 **cup pecans, chopped**
1 **teaspoon vanilla**
1/2 **teaspoon salt**

Preheat oven to 325°.

Cream butter; add sugar. Stir thoroughly and add flour, salt, nuts and vanilla. Shape into balls or crescents and bake on ungreased cookie sheet for 20 minutes or until light brown.

Roll in confectioner's sugar while warm.

Yields 4 dozen

Mary's Sand Tarts

Cold-Oven Pound Cake

Cold-Oven
Pound Cake

This is very easy to make. Good anytime—
breakfast, dinner or supper!

$1^1/_2$ **cups butter**
$2^1/_2$ **cups sugar**
5 eggs
$3^3/_4$ **cups flour**
$1/_8$ **teaspoon salt**
$1/_4$ **teaspoon baking powder**
1 cup milk
1 teaspoon vanilla

Mix dry ingredients together, divide. Cream butter and
sugar. Add eggs individually, mixing after each addition.
Add half the dry ingredients. Add milk and vanilla. Add
remaining half the dry ingredients and beat for 1 minute.
Pour into a well-greased tube pan. Put cake into cold oven
and turn to 325°. Bake for $1^1/_2$ hours or until knife inserted in
center comes out clean.

Turn out after 10 minutes and pour hot icing over hot cake.

ICING
1 cup sugar
$1/_2$ **cup butter**
$1/_4$ **cup water**
$1/_4$ **cup rum**
$1/_4$ **cup lemon or lime juice**
lemon or lime zest

Combine all ingredients in saucepan. Boil 2 to 3 minutes.
Pour over hot cake. Sprinkle with zest.

 Serves 12

Texas
Cheesecake

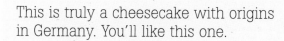

This is truly a cheesecake with origins
in Germany. You'll like this one.

$1/_2$ **recipe Dutch Oven Delight Dough,** *recipe page 180*
4 cups cottage cheese, drained
1 cup sour cream
2 tablespoons (scant) cornstarch
juice of 1 lemon
$1/_2$ **cup sugar (or more to taste)**
3 eggs, lightly beaten
1 teaspoon almond or lemon extract
1 cup raisins

Prepare Dutch Oven Delight Dough. After dough has doubled
in bowl, roll it out to $1/_2$-inch thickness; place into 16-inch
Dutch oven or on a 12 x 18-inch baking sheet. Set aside to
rise in a warm place for 45 minutes.

In large mixing bowl, combine cottage cheese with sour
cream, then stir in remaining ingredients. Spread cheese mixture on top of risen dough. Bake 40 minutes at 325 to 350°.
When done, brush with browned butter and sprinkle with
sugar.

Serves 12

Dutch Oven
Delight

This is a typical cowboy dessert—heavy on flour and sugar. Oldtimers tell the story of a cowboy who'd been riding fencelines away from headquarters all winter. He rode in one day—probably hadn't had anything sweet in months-and proceeded to make Bear Sign. It was such a hit that he became the cook. We offer three sweet variations that are great for a Sunday brunch.

DUTCH OVEN DELIGHT DOUGH

2 cups milk, scalded	2 teaspoons salt
2 2-ounce packages yeast or 6 $^1/_4$-ounce packets dry yeast	2 eggs, beaten
	2 teaspoons vanilla
$^3/_4$ cup shortening	6 cups flour
$^1/_4$ cup butter	melted butter
$^1/_2$ cup sugar	1 tablespoon cinnamon mixed with 2 cups sugar

Preheat oven to 350°.

To scalded milk, add 1 tablespoon sugar; sprinkle yeast on top and let stand to soften. In a mixing bowl, cream shortening and butter, add remaining sugar and salt. Cream all until light and fluffy. Add beaten eggs, mix. Add yeast mixture, vanilla and enough flour to yield soft dough. Work with a spoon until smooth and elastic. Knead lightly on floured surface. Place dough in greased bowl, cover and let rise until doubled, about 1 hour.

Pinch off balls as you would for sourdough biscuits. Dip each ball in melted butter, then cinnamon-sugar. Crowd into well-greased 14-inch Dutch oven. Let rise until doubled, 30 to 45 minutes. Bake for 25 to 30 minutes.

Serves 12

Bear Sign

OR for Maple Twist

FILLING
1/2 cup sugar
1 teaspoon cinnamon
1 teaspoon maple flavoring
1/3 cup pecans, chopped

GLAZE
11/2 cups confectioner's sugar
1/4 teaspoon maple flavoring
2 to 3 tablespoons milk

Pinch off three 3-inch balls. On floured surface, roll each
ball to 1/8-inch thickness. Place one piece on 12-inch nonstick
pizza pan. Brush dough with 2 tablespoons melted butter and
sprinkle with one-third of the filling. Repeat, ending with filling on top. With a glass, mark a 2-inch circle in dough's center; do not cut through. Cut from outside edge just to center
circle, forming 16 pie-shaped wedges. Twist each of the
three-layered wedges five times. Let rise in warm place 45
minutes. Bake at 375° for 25 minutes. Drizzle with glaze.

Makes two twists

OR for Bear Sign

Pinch off dough in egg-sized balls, then roll into 3/4- to 1-inch
logs. Let rise 15 minutes. Deep fry as you would doughnuts;
coat with sugar-cinnamon mixture. Serve hot.

Yields 35 to 40 rolls

Side-Saddle Pecan Addiction

Side-Saddle
Pecan Addiction

You are going to hate us for giving you this recipe because you can't quit eating it.

CRUST
2 cups flour
1 cup butter
1 cup sugar
1/2 teaspoon salt

Preheat oven to 350°.

Melt butter and place in large mixing bowl. Add dry ingredients and mix. Spray 9 x 13-inch pan, or 10-inch round, deep cake pan with nonstick spray. Spread crust in pan and bake for 20 minutes until crust is puffy and light brown. Remove from oven and press down fluffy spots and corners.

FILLING
12 eggs, beaten
2 cups brown sugar
1 cup Karo light syrup
1 cup sorghum molasses or maple syrup
1/2 cup + 1 tablespoon flour
4 1/2 cups pecan pieces
1 tablespoon vanilla

Combine eggs, brown sugar, syrup and molasses. Stir until smooth. Add flour and stir until well blended and smooth. Stir in pecans and vanilla. Pour filling in crust and bake 45 minutes at 360°.

 Serves 12

USING LINERS

One of the tricks Bill Cauble has learned while cooking with Dutch ovens is to use heavy cake pans as liners for the Dutch oven. Sugar will burn and stick to the cast iron pans, so the liners allow you to use the Dutch oven for cakes and pies. Too, you can pour water into the Dutch oven, then place the liner in and add ingredients for casseroles or other main dishes.

Homemade
Vanilla Ice Cream

No matter what, nothing compares to homemade ice cream. Though not many hand-cranked ice cream freezers remain, many have fond memories of sitting atop the freezer as it was being cranked or cranking it yourself. The harder it was to turn, the nearer you were to a sweet treat.

1½ quarts milk
6 eggs, beaten
14-ounce can of sweetened condensed milk
1 teaspoon salt
¾ cup sugar
1 tablespoon flour
1 pint half-and-half
1½ tablespoons vanilla

Heat 1 quart of milk to scalding while combining salt, sugar and flour. Add dry mixture to eggs and mix. Add to milk, stirring constantly until it thickens. Remove from heat; add sweetened condensed milk. Cool. Pour into ice cream freezer can and add remaining milk, half-and-half and vanilla. Freeze.

TIP: If you have fresh fruit or nuts, add them before freezing.

 Yields 3 to 4 quarts

Overnight
Apricot Cake

This is another cookoff-winning dessert. When preparing this and other desserts in Dutch ovens, we always use aluminum pans to line the insides of the ovens.

4 cups flour, sifted
1 teaspoon salt
1 tablespoon sugar
1 cup shortening
1 2-ounce cake yeast or 3 ¼-ounce packets dry yeast
1 cup cold milk
3 egg yolks, beaten
12 ounces dried apricots
½ cup sugar

FILLING
3 egg whites, beaten stiff
1 cup sugar
1 teaspoon cinnamon

Preheat oven to 325°.

Sift dry ingredients together; cut in shortening. Dissolve yeast in warm milk, add to dry ingredients. Add beaten egg yolks. Mix; do not knead. Cover and refrigerate overnight.

Cover apricots with water and simmer until soft. Add ½ cup sugar and mash with fork.

Mix together filling ingredients.

Separate dough into three parts, roll each to ¼-inch thickness. Place one in 3 x 10-inch greased liner pan. Spread one-third of the apricots over dough; add one-third of the filling. Add another layer of dough, more apricots and filling. Repeat with apricots and filling on top.

Place liner pan in Dutch oven and bake 35 to 40 minutes.

 Serves 10

Bourbon Sauce

This Bourbon Sauce is a luscious accompaniment to Bread Pudding. Rum or brandy can be substituted for a variation.

1 cup sugar
1/2 cup unsalted butter
1/2 cup half-and-half
1/4 cup Jack Daniel's Black Label Tennessee Whiskey
1 teaspoon vanilla

Combine ingredients in a medium saucepan and bring to low boil, cooking until thickened. Pour warm sauce over bread pudding 30 minutes before serving, or spoon over individual servings as they are served. Sauce may be kept refrigerated for one week and reheated. It's good over ice cream.

Yields 1 1/2 cups

Bourbon Sauce

INDEX

Numerals in italics indicate an illustration of the subject mentioned.

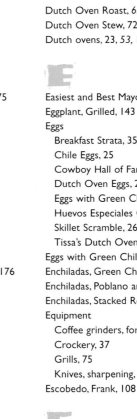

ACKNOWLEDGMENTS

Bill Cauble and Clifford Teinert

We extend special thanks to Tommy Lee Jones, who understands the importance of the chuck wagon's position in history, and to Bill Wittliff for his photograph of Tommy Lee. We thank Sonja Irwin Clayton for the use of the essay on chuck wagon history written by Lawrence Clayton, her late husband and our friend.

We appreciate the authentic backdrop provided by Lambshead Ranch and Collins Creek Ranch. We thank the Matthews family for welcoming us during this project.

For sharing his photographic talent, we are grateful to Watt Casey, Jr. And we thank the following people for lending us their photographic presence in this book: Donnie Baize, Tom Belcher, Art Berry, Jaime Camacho, John Caldwell, Larry Cauble, Ernie Davis, Jim Davis, Dale Deaton, Billy Estridge, Bob Favor, Arthur Garcia, Guy Gillette, Pip Gillette, Rusty Gilbert, Dick Hash, Jimbo Humphreys, Matt Humphreys, Will Humphreys, Lee Johnson, Ardon Judd, Bud Lowrey, Lester Lofton, Terry Moberley, Jamie Nail, George Peacock, Skip Rhoades, Angel Rosales, John Snyder, Lynne Teinert and Bobby Willliams.

We thank Teresa Clemmer, Betty Law and Sally Stapp for sharing plates, platters and props. We thank Bob Echols and Prissy Harvick of Albany, and Craig Winters of the Nail Ranch near Albany.

For tenaciously pushing, pulling and guiding us, we thank Rue Judd of Bright Sky Press. And for helping us pull the pieces together by capturing our thoughts, voices, and way of cooking, we are grateful to our editor, Katie Dickie Stavinoha, and to Sunday Belcher Kornyé.

We thank our fathers, Jay Cauble and John Teinert, for making sure we learned the time-honored traditions of preparing and barbecuing meat. We thank our mothers, Liz Cauble and Edna Teinert, for their love and encouragement.

Finally, for their patience, prodding, advice and good humor throughout the writing of this book, we thank our wives, Doris Cauble and Lynne Teinert.

Watt Casey, Jr.—I wish to express deepest gratitude to my wife Shelley, my parents and immediate family, my extended family, and a handful of close friends, all of whom have given their support and encouragement through the years.

For sharing their archival photographs, I am grateful to the Panhandle-Plains Historical Museum in Canyon, Texas, and to The Heart of West Texas Museum in Colorado City, Texas.

I thank Curtis Rister, Deryl Clark, Stan West and his crew at Photo Image Center, River City Silver, and Brookshire's Grocery in Albany. I thank HEB and Central Market for the beautiful produce and food used in many of the featured recipes. I thank Bill and Clifford for making it easy and fun. I thank Bright Sky Press—Rue Judd, Kate Hartson and Carol Cates for their vision—and Rue for her never-ending enthusiasm.